PREACHING AND THE MIND OF TODAY

PREACHING
and the Mind of Today

By
GAIUS GLENN ATKINS

ROUND TABLE PRESS, INC.
New York   1934

PRINTED IN THE UNITED STATES OF AMERICA BY
SELECT PRINTING COMPANY, INC., NEW YORK, N. Y.

Dedication

"Books," so Francis Bacon wrote in the dedication of his own book to a king, "ought to have no patrons but truth and reason," but most authors, having neither the courage nor the conceit to dedicate their efforts to patrons so severe, have wisely chosen kindlier tribunals.

THIS BOOK IS DEDICATED TO MY STUDENT COMRADES OF THE CLASSROOM IN HOMILETICS DURING THE LAST EIGHT YEARS

with the confident expectation that, if they here discover familiar matter, they will emulate the admirable example of the generous-minded Greeks, who, according to Rudyard Kipling, when they recognized even in Homer what they had often heard before, made no unpleasantness about it, nor any fuss—

"But winked at 'Omer down the road,
And 'e winked back—the same as us."

THE AUTHOR'S APOLOGY FOR HIS BOOK

THERE is no reason in its etymology why an apology should be either a defense or a retraction. It simply means that one keeps on talking—or writing—about what he has already said or written—a blameless and entirely human habit without which conversation would languish and letters be impoverished. Indeed the apologies of our wisest and best, through the wealth of experience upon which they comment, have become our treasured possessions. If Socrates had not spoken as he did of his own life after he had drunk the hemlock, literature would lack a classic; if John Henry Newman had not written an Apologia—which was anything but an apology—he would never have been a Prince of the Church.

Most autobiographies are, I think, motivated by some desire of those about whom the world has said many things to have the last word as near as may be themselves. If, therefore, a word of such eminent descent and respectable use has come to suggest the acknowledgment of a fault rather than what the French call *éclaircissement,* it is rather because of its long association with our fallible human nature than its own character. Only the elect, of whom there have never been many, can keep on talking about what they have already said without the sense of some need either to explain why they did not say it better, or else to add what they fondly believe will make it more complete. This, I think, may as justly be attributed to our passion for a finer artistry as to our sins of omission and commission. This is why most authors write introductions to their books.

No author has more need of some kind of an apologia than the man who now writes a book on any phase of preaching, for no subject has been more exhaustively and variously considered by men who both illustrate and adorn the vocation they discuss. I have tried in the first chapter to account for the quantity and quality of the literature on preaching. It is the elusiveness of the vocation which has in part created the literature about it and which by a subtle compensation always makes another book about it possible, whether it be needed or not. Almost every preacher has an urge to enlarge upon his calling; every teacher of preaching is quite sure in his more sanguine moments that there is a wisdom in his notes for which his fellow-craftsmen are waiting. This particular book has grown out of the author's classroom work, his happy contacts with many groups of preachers in conferences and "Summer Schools," his own experience as a preacher, and, very greatly, the situation in which preaching finds itself today in its relation to the general mind of the time.

Preaching is trying valiantly to re-relate itself to an order which needs what preaching might do almost desperately and confuses every effort by the complexity of its factors. The rise and extension of key words which, being used in one connection, prove so useful that thereafter they are borrowed and used in many fields is always a fascinating study. Such words come in on tides of need and insight, and so register significant movements in strategic regions. They are not the movements themselves any more than the weather-vane is the wind or the buoy the tide; they come and go with the great changing currents of the human enterprise.

"Re-thinking" is just now one of our most significant phrases. It can be used in connection with almost any great department of human concern, for most things about us need to be re-thought, and most of all those aspects of our common life which reflect the emergence of changed and changing forces, conditions, or understandings. Static situations do not much need to be taken back into the general mind and reconsidered—at least they do not get taken back into the general mind and reconsidered; which may be why we are so often caught unawares by the breaking up of orders which have seemed so blessedly permanent. Long established concerns of any sort not only seem to make re-thinking unnecessary, they strongly object to being re-thought. It is likely to be unsettling and with the best will in the world sure to be critical. It is a demanding task never quickly or easily carried through, and to an age like ours obsessed with action and impatient of slow processes of examination it seems futile and remote.

But when inherited orders begin to register portentous strains before the impact of emerging forces, they demand to be taken back into the mind again and there recast. There is no other way and no other place to begin. That is what minds are for and to refuse thus to use them is to deny the efficiency of the one instrument which is our first resource, the secret of all our power, the enablement of all our hope. It is also to imperil the very enterprises which we refuse to re-think. The very confusions which attend hard-driven transition periods, the race against time which is the one outstanding aspect of our present estate complicate every process of re-thinking but they only make the need of it more urgent.

Re-thinking anything today along with all its other difficulties has, curiously enough, to reckon with the psychologist. He is just now engaged in proving that reason is only a veneer on the surface of elemental urgencies and always open to suspicion. He reaches his conclusions through more or less subtle reasonings of his own but that is another matter. Our task, he thinks, is to discover, capture, and redirect the forces which really control us. This may be true enough but in the end it does no more than prove that the psychologist is re-thinking human nature. If the forces which really control us are to be redirected, we still seem to need some reasonable understanding of the ends toward which they should be redirected and how we shall set about it.

How all this bears upon our social and economic situations and everything from our own thresholds to the seven seas which involves human relationships is a commonplace. No one can say yet how wisely or creatively this re-thinking is being done. We do know that all our efforts are crossed and recrossed with heat and haste. That we are more concerned for some immediate advantage than for the distant common good. That partisanship, heady self-justifications, the enormous inertia of the established, and the magnitude of the undertaking involve all our action is a dusty murk. Where men ought to think they protest and indict. But the task goes on. It must.

*   *   *

Just at the heart of it all are the Christian church and the Christian pulpit, charged with a double task: to re-think themselves and to furnish the individual and society the ruling ideas under whose illuminating control they may creatively re-think all the meanings, values, and ends of life. A church with no clear sense of its own mission, which has not like St. Paul been "laid hold on" by a divine mandate whose full realization is always beyond its power but toward the attainment of which it presses on and reaches out, is not likely to lay hold creatively of any situation. It will spend its force upon itself or else, since it is uncertain of the great ends, be going off hotfoot on crusades and drives for minor offensives entirely worthy and pathetically inadequate. With every qualification demanded by the recognition of the invaluable service the church has rendered and is rendering, with the full recognition of the vision and wisdom of its leaders, this is in substance what American Protestantism has been doing for a long generation, and the results have been what they have been.*

It is true that movements which seek an entirely Christian objective are progressing. We are moving toward social justice, beyond social first-aid to the injured toward a surer sense of what is really doing the damage, beyond political device toward an arresting recognition of what is wrong in the very structure of social and economic orders. If all the resolutions passed by Church Assemblies should become the resolute will of Christian folk, we should not be far from the kingdom of God. But there has always been an uncaptured region behind every position taken. The master-control still escapes us.

The church *is* clarifying its conception of its immediate task; it is re-thinking its present state and its sovereign responsibilities, and it has enough to re-think. Within a long generation practically the whole content of inherited Christianity has come up for re-examination, asked to be taken back into the Christian mind and re-issued, charged with proper power and meaning for its contemporaneous world. Preaching cannot escape that challenge. On the contrary it should rejoice in it for the abundance of material thus supplied if for no other reason. It cannot re-think its own function without re-thinking religion, the Christian gospel, the meaning of that gospel for the time, and the time itself. Centrally its task seems almost unbelievably clear and insistent: *To create a Christian mind, taking "mind" in its most ample sense, which will accept and commit itself to the*

---

* In spite of all reassuring statistics as to numerical growth, there is plenty to challenge the church to thoughtful self-examination. Since this book was written Roger Babson and a Commission on Church Attendance have furnished figures which bear out definitely certain "undocumented" statements in the book. A study of 1,400 churches shows that in churches with an average membership of 322, with an average seating capacity of 370, only 25 per cent are active members, and only 30 per cent of the seats occupied. The disconcerting spread between the quality of our common life and the Christian standard cannot be put in figures but it is there.

Christian way with all which the Christian way involves and demands. There is the still untaken citadel. Western civilization professes a Christian faith; it lacks too largely a Christian mind and will.

*　　*　　*

One of our brilliant political "realists" has just been saying in a current magazine article that the relative failure of all the machinery set up for international peace is due (in substance) to the minds and motives of those who speak and act for the nations. They are all seeking ends entirely incompatible with international peace so—what's the use? All this was said at length with a really sound analysis and those nuances of style by no means delicate which commend articles to editors. The writer reserved his sharpest thrusts for the sentimental and "tender-hearted" who object to his particular type of realism, in short, for current Christian idealism and idealists, though, as far as I remember, he did not use the word Christian.

Well, there are Christians who quite agree with him in substance though they take a different line. They are more inclined to urge the unescapable limits against which any idealism beats itself out, or else the futility of it unless it create for itself a machinery through which it can function. Just now the church as a whole is most interested in creating the mechanism. There is no question here of "either—or." Our current traffic of every sort cannot be carried on one track, least of all the Realm of God.

But behind all the many-mindedness of the time, above all hotly contested positions, the final condition of every program is a social mind entirely competent to carry it. Minorities may for a season impose their program upon divisively minded majorities. A nation may through a cumulative appeal be brought for a little to some idealistic position far above the levels of its usual life; as though a wave should at last register high above the level of the sea. But then——? The sea level is always there and the wave comes back to it.

Something is commonly gained. Prohibition has come and gone but the state is for the time more sober and the gravest abuses of the traffic in drink have not yet reappeared. Conditions which have heretofore mobilized armies do not now compel the fatal word. Peace is being maintained and, one would like to believe, advanced by slow-shaping, half-hidden forces which will some day be recognized as actually the emergence of a changed national and international mind. Whatever contributes to the making of it will have right to share its triumph. But in the long run no advance can be imposed upon a majority of unprepared or hostile minds, and the whole tendency of the time is to impose and not to evoke. That is the dictator's philosophy and, lately, his red-handed policy. He may secure acquiescence or brief seeming consent, he might in the end secure for his philosophy and power a supporting general mind but all the demonstrations of experience are against him. Until, in St. Paul's great phrase again, the spirit of the mind is reached and changed, all enterprises ride uncertain seas. This would seem to be the task of the Christian church and the outstanding function of Christian preaching: to renew the spirit of the mind.

*   *   *

It is out of this simple, time-worn thesis that this book was written. I did not mean to write it that way. I began with rather much used analyses of the mind of the time for a "scenario"; that the mind of the time was cynical, disillusioned, secular, realistic, confused, disoriented, questing, of enormous pregnant power; that preaching should direct itself toward the correction of which is wrong in the modern mind and the reinforcement of what is right. And there were all my chapters: Preaching to a cynical age, a disillusioned age and so on to the end, depending upon one's ingenuity and resource. A book like that should write itself. As a matter of fact it did not. Some of the chapters began to be out-dated before I got them finished. The times are no longer cynical; they have accepted their disillusionments. They are secular enough, just how forceful they are remains to be seen. I began to see that my proposed chapter headings would deal with the mood rather than the mind of the time. That what we call the phases of our mind were really our moods. That contemporaneous preaching was too concerned about the moods when it should be shaping a more creative mind. That in vital regions the Christian mind, by the elemental tests of the mind of Jesus Christ, was still too largely to create.

The real trouble seemed to be the unevenness of the current Christian mind. Here there was actually a Christian mind, there it lagged disastrously but everywhere it appeared to be the key to every other position. Through all these regions—demanding, embattled, filled with hot movement, and strangely empty—I began, as I went on, to see the outlines of such a field for preaching as it has never had before. The terrain opened up, its horizons lay far and challenging. It was the terrain of human need and confusion, of appealing folk who moved bravely, pathetically, questingly through tasks which had lost their meaning and endeavors which found a poor issue compared with their unfulfilled splendor. Then I knew how Jesus was moved with compassion when He looked upon the multitudes—sheep without a shepherd—and how He charged His own: "Feed my sheep."

But no one could make a book of that either. It was too big —and, bafflingly enough, too simple. It was as though one should offer the multiplication table as a rather startling discovery. And yet there was something startling about it—that we should have been so slow to find out that two and two make four; that the Way and the Truth and the Life of Jesus Christ are the supreme wisdom of life and that we are still so foolish.

*　　*　　*

So the book finally took its own line; not too easily, not adequately, with many detours which had to be left out, and with a haunting sense of saying the obvious, qualified only by the conviction that what was obvious for Jesus because it was sovereign is obvious for us only because we have heard it so often and done so little about it. Just now what is more needed than anything else under the stars is the general persuasion that the Christian way is so obvious that we have no alternative to it. If preaching knew how to make the obvious of Jesus as splendid as it really is, preaching would be re-clothed with power. And I came to this conclusion; that as far as preaching is failing or has failed it is because it has not the splendid simplicity of the mind of Christ.

I do not see how all this can be driven in upon today's need except as it begins with today's situations, whether they be sick or puzzled souls, a sick or a puzzled society. Here is the whole front of what folk are and know and do and miss and seek, and here beyond every inch of it from the shadow—or the light—across our own thresholds to the challenge of a confused world whose trumpets sound along all the far-flung line, is a demand for the message and empowerment of the Christian gospel. Who could not preach in a time like this? Which is all I have tried to say.

I have used little direct quotation though naturally many sources of suggestion. The work is in debt to The Macmillan Company for their generous permission to quote from Rabindranath Tagore *The Religion of Man,* and William DeWitt Hyde *The Five Great Philosophies of Life.*

What is under-said or over-said the reader, being most likely a preacher himself, will properly qualify. What is omitted is not therefore denied; what is unfinished other minds will take and finish. The book does not end; it just stops. I had in mind a final chapter on the preacher himself but the publisher said it would be one chapter too many and, moreover, Dr. William Jewett Tucker's Yale Lectures on the *Making and Unmaking of the Preacher* have said all that with a final wisdom accessible to any reader. I know enough of my present task as a teacher of preaching to know that one more book about preaching is—just one more book about preaching, so why not stop when one is through. Much of what is here said I said in substance lately to a most gracious group of men in Pastors Schools of the Southern Methodist Church. Their response leads me a little to hope that here and there a fellow-craftsman will find something for which he cares.

GAIUS GLENN ATKINS.

Auburn Theological Seminary
Huntington House
July 26, 1934.

TABLE OF CONTENTS

CHAPTER I

THE STRANGE VOCATION OF
PREACHING

THE last United States Census of Religious Bodies reported 232,154 churches of all denominations, exclusive of Jewish congregations, with 54,576,346 members or communicants. Almost half the population is connected with the 215 major and minor denominations which, with other religious groups—some of them of a highly experimental nature—serve the soul of America. There is a wide variation of conditions among the churches and denominations. A study of Protestant churches, just released, estimates 85,000 of them to be too weak in membership and resource to function properly. The Congregational-Christian denomination (a rather stable group) reports —out of a total of 6,379 churches—312 with less than ten members and 1,672 with less than fifty; reduced to percentages these figures are likely to be fairly representative. The census includes marginal groups the conduct of whose meetings may vary from waiting for a message from the discarnate to going into the silence. Generalization is thus difficult, but with few exceptions they all have on thing in common: "preaching."

The census furnishes no statistics about the number of sermons delivered on any given Sunday, or the number of the faithful who listen to them. No census could. The Roman Catholic church organizes its worship around the celebration of the mass. The Friend may sit in creative quietness, moved by the spirit only to be still. Liturgical Protestantism makes preaching subsidiary to worship and the sacraments but its clergy continue to preach. For the vast majority of evangelical Protestant churches the sermon is the thing. Some form of address is pretty sure to accompany meetings of Theosophical and Vedanta societies, Pentecostal Assemblies of the Word, Defenseless Mennonites, Daniel's Band, the Hepzibah Faith Missionary Association, and the Pillar of Fire. Christian Science churches maintain a board of lecturers. At least one mass of a Sunday in Roman Catholic churches is followed by a sermon. That church has in addition its preaching missions and its preaching orders carefully chosen and tirelessly trained.

No church needs to go without a sermon for want of a preacher. The over-multiplied Protestant theological seminaries plead, in asking support from reluctant constituencies, a dearth of ministers. The number of applicants for any vacant pulpit must lead church officials and committees to doubt the validity of that plea. There are probably at present more reasonably well trained men than churches to support them, with a margin of poorly trained and precariously supported ministers who are a source of anxiety to themselves, their denominational boards, and Protestantism as a whole. Churches too poor to maintain a minister of their own are "yoked" together—and occasionally find the yoke galling. Such as these may be preached to only twice a month or even once. But since most churches in the more representative communions hear two sermons on Sunday and a camouflaged sermon at their "midweek meeting" or prayer meeting, it is rather safe to assume, if one adds the synagogues, rescue missions, revival campaigns, and the like, that over 200,000 sermons and religious addresses are delivered in America every week.

The entire membership of the American churches is never present, it is also safe to assume, on any given Sunday. The smaller churches may, and generally do, have an average attendance equal to their membership—this is applied to Protestant churches only—the larger churches certainly do not. If one-third the total membership of the American churches are in attendance at any one time, at least 18,000,000 people listen to sermons—or their equivalent—every week. With a fifteen per cent margin of variation either way, being preached to is one of the principal indoor occupations of the American people.

They may come eagerly or with some measure of urging, but essentially they come of their own free choice. The desire to hear a sermon is by no means their only compelling motive. Loyalty to their church, the quest for God, habit, the mystic summons of the sacrament, the inspiration of worship, escape from the routine of colorless lives, and the timeless appeal of religion all combine to assemble congregations. But if the sermon were taken out of representative Protestant worship the keystone of its arch would be gone, and Roman Catholicism without preaching would lose one of the buttresses of its mighty structure. It is this centrality of preaching not only in Christian churches but in liberal Judaism which gives to any consideration of it a perennial significance. There is no vocation about which, as concerns the exercise of it, more has been said and written. Books about preaching fill whole alcoves in the libraries of every theological seminary.

I.

No other profession has anything quite parallel to this. The doctor has a highly specialized and always growing literature dealing with every aspect of medical science, the most minute detail of every possible operation, and whatever else is included in the conduct of his noble profession. But it is nearly all objective. He has doubtless been instructed about his bedside manners and the rather demanding etiquette of the profession.

He takes the oath of Hippocrates; but no one addresses him glowingly on the "Romance of the Practice of Medicine" or writes him a book about the "Foolishness of Being a Doctor," * though without doubt either title would occasionally be apropos. The doctor's personality is an important factor in his success or failure, but his main concern is to make himself the finely disciplined instrument of a very great science. His books deal centrally with his science and its technique and not with the practitioner.

The main concern of the lawyer is with the corpus of the law common and statute; trial procedure, precedents and decisions, and the fundamental law of constitutions written or unwritten. He is trained in nice discrimination, soundness of detached judgment; at his best, in clear and weighty utterance. He must know how to win decisions from the bench and verdicts from the jury. He must have an explicit or implicit psychology of argument and appeal. He must sense the emotional actions and reactions of those twelve men in a jury box whose power over property, liberty, and life has been generally —and perhaps erroneously—considered the supreme achievement of the common law. But, for all that, the practice of law is subject to a rigid objective control. The grave, leather-bound books in the lawyer's library contain no long series of "Chancellor Kent Lectures" on the art and elusiveness of his profession.

Teaching has an extensive and authoritative literature not entirely alien to the literature on preaching since what the teacher does is communicated through personality far more than the lawyer's opinion or the doctor's conduct of a case. But directly the science of teaching passes beyond generalities it becomes the technique of teaching *something*—arithmetic or language, geometry or physics. If this specific procedure in definite subjects were taken out of pedagogy, it would be left

* Adaptation of titles of books on preaching.

raveled and undone. The subjective area in teaching is both considerable and significant, but it has a factual control which gives definiteness to all its literature.

II.

The arts, it would seem, are still more subjective. The painter makes the picture, the sculptor the statue, and the musician the song. Preaching is also an art and, as we shall presently see, the laws which govern all art govern preaching—or should; but while it seems to be assumed that a very great deal can be done for preachers by lecturing them about preaching, no amount of being lectured to will ever make a painter. He is far more likely to be inspired by a picture which seems to him a perfect expression of his art than by anything the most acute critic can say about it or by earnest exhortation to paint like that himself.

I am not questioning the value of acute criticism in art. The really valuable literature in that field is always essentially interpretative, analytical, and critical. There will be an exhaustive examination of composition, the handling of lights and shadows, color values, brush-work, how the empty spaces are managed— an unexpectedly significant affair which the preacher should also consider—where the highlights should fall, and all such aspects of El Greco's "Assumption," Franz Hal's "Man with a Glove," Millet's "Man with a Hoe," or the last highly impressionistic blur on canvas. But painters are not thus taught to paint. Their teacher may point a fault with the handle of his brush or correct an inept space with a master touch, but an artist learns to paint by rubbing out and trying again till his genius is evoked and empowered by tireless toil. There is for him, when all is said and done, only one rule, the rule of a great French teacher: *"Continuez, mes enfants."*

One might expect in music a literature more nearly comparable to the preacher's books on preaching since music is always a fusion of personality and performance. This, of course, applies only to rendition. The printed score of Beethoven's 5th Symphony or Bach's Grand Mass are as objective as a picture, a book, or a pile of brick. But they can be expressed as music only through the musician. They are played as much upon the instrumentation of his mind and emotions as upon his organ or his violin; the overtones are the creation of his spirit, and his temperament colors the interpretation. Gabrilowitsch conducts the Detroit Symphony as a pianist, playing upon wood-winds, brasses, and strings as he plays the piano. Isaye conducted the Cincinnati Orchestra as a violinist, evoking broad singing tones and making a violin string even of the cymbals and drums.

Vocal music is still more subjective; it is the singer's art asking through the singer a recognition without which it could not exist. His need to know at once, in some form of acknowledgment, whether what he has done has "gone across" is not altogether temperamental self-centeredness. For the moment, the singer is the song. Here the preacher and the musician are much alike save that the preacher is not only the soloist but commonly composes the song. The parson at the foot of the pulpit stairs ostensibly greeting his flock but actually waiting for some heartening comment upon what he has just done is, like the musician, in that expectant attitude through some deep necessity of his vocation. He has spent upon the silence a travail of his mind and spirit, which have become for one high hour the channel of something vaster than himself. He cannot go on if his word returns to him void.

For all that, there is no literature on being a musician comparable with the shelves of books on preaching. One will also look in vain to the library of the engineer or architect for anything approaching it. Preaching stands alone in the range and variety of the literature dealing, not with its content, but with its conduct. The only possible explanation of this must be in the nature of preaching itself. It has its controls in theology and church authority; it moves within the wide and elastic frontiers of the Christian religion; it inherits from generation to generation a recognized subject matter, but when everything else is said preaching remains the lonely adventure of the preacher into the unseen. He is always asking for a map, and no map can quite assure him of reaching the goal. His true guide-posts are in his own mind and spirit. By any test the business of being a preacher is a strange business.

III.

It is nothing more or less than the creation by the spoken word of some sense of the presence of God and reality of religion. It seeks to fill the void of human loneliness "with the sound of solitary voices" proclaiming the unseen and eternal, to lighten our darkness with the uncreated light. Such a definition of preaching is too indefinite to be sound but it offers a point of departure and explains the long ascendancy of preaching in Protestantism and its tenacious significance in Latin Catholicism. And it would, through the very indefiniteness of it, account for the preacher's wearing concern for his elusive craft, his eager quest for help and the bewildering variety of proffered help. All books about preaching are by preachers themselves.* They can hardly be classified as confessional literature, though the confession element is always implicit in them, colors them delicately or otherwise, and is generally the secret of what real power they possess.

They are a sharing of experience as though the men who,

---

* Only one volume, I think, in the Lyman Beecher Series is by a layman. Since the laity supply the congregation, their mind about preaching might be well worth getting. As far, however, as it has been ascertained by questionnaires and the like, the result has not been helpful.

by one test or another, have been most successful in finding a road through the hopes and fears, the dreams and assurances which constitute the preacher's country should, from what heights they have gained, say to their brethren: "These are the roads——." What they say is heard or read and pondered by the questing in the hope that, having found the secret of so rare a power, they may exercise it themselves. But alas, though the formulæ may be told, the precipitate in the crucible, like the elixir of life, never quite bestows the coveted gift. For it is in its final essence uncommunicable.

What can be taught about preaching as an art never reaches its mystic sources. This inability, which we will not confess to ourselves, to reach the true hiding place of its power is likely the secret of our excessive concern for the technique of it. An early occupant of the chair which the writer holds was called "Professor of Sacred Rhetoric." Just what makes rhetoric sacred is a nice question. Mr. Wells says that the two women in Titian's "Sacred and Profane Love" are the same, the difference, which is considerable, being in what they do or do not wear. The differences between "sacred" and "profane" rhetoric would seem to be in the subjects considered and the ends sought, and not in the general laws of the right use of language. (One is tempted to believe that "sacred rhetoric" has often taken the overdressed part.) Creative disciplines of method and style in public address belong to the general field of education.

Significantly enough, the highly specialized emphasis upon the art of preaching in theological education and the excess of supplementary books and lectures are peculiarly American. English churches—Anglican or Free—have no such specialization. Their leaders are given a training in literature, history, and philosophy rarely equaled in American theological seminaries or colleges, and left to preach very largely by the light of nature out of a full and instructed mind. The English preachers who are invited to lecture upon American foundations are themselves the product of this discipline and witnesses to its efficiency. American specialization in homiletic training is probably due in part to the uneven and sometimes deficient background education of American preachers. It reflects also the strain American preaching is under, of creating the congregation and carrying the back-breaking burden of over-institutionalized and over-financed churches in an over-churched nation. It is not due to some esoteric quality in "sacred rhetoric."

No one else delivers himself so often or continuously as a preacher, but there are effective speakers in every field with no training beyond a disciplined mind whose work will easily stand comparison with that of any preacher. The great English parliamentarians have had a faculty and power which few English preachers have attained. American political address has never had the noble and mellow simplicity of the best English public address, but it will have held its own with preaching. The best writing on the finer aspects of the difficult art of living is being done today by men who have seen theological seminaries only from a distance, very much as Newman in a famous passage said he had seen, after he left Littlemore, the towers and spires of Oxford. Nor have they felt, as he felt, the pathos of that brief and distant view.

Evidently, then, preaching is something more than effective public speech, or else the constant demand for guidance in the technique of it is a sad witness that we have missed the fundamentals of good training even in that. I think both alternatives are true, but the nature of preaching itself is far the most significant. Its sense of being charged with a commission for those supreme interests of the soul by which men live, for want of which they die, is—or should be—the unescapable and awesome burden of all preaching, and that burden is not easily borne.

IV.

The altar and the pulpit have been from the very beginning of Christianity its two great instruments, but they did not begin with Christianity. There are older altars, less seemly, behind every Christian altar; there are very ancient inheritances behind every sermon. Preaching, like everything else, cannot be understood apart from its genesis. It began in the necessity that any corporate human enterprise must in certain stages of it become a word or words. There may be, likely are, inarticulate depths in human nature, urgencies older than any name for them, more persistent than any rationalization of them, and all our human ways may stem from these hidden roots which are the nature of us and for which no words are ever adequate. But they never issue in any action involving human relationship unless they be made real in words and carried through and on by words.

Religion naturally needs words also. It may become too much an affair with words and, through the detachment of its words from life, become perilously unreal. It has always had other voices than the preacher's; some of them more true to its genius than the preacher's voice can ever be. The poet's was the first voice of religion (it might be the last, singing a requiem in "the graveyard of dead creeds"). The wonder of religion, its appeal to the imagination, its need to play upon the heartstrings were the poet's birthright. He saw the goddess of the dawn issue from the dark, heard the tumultuous passing of the storm-gods and made a music of them, a music older than any creed, more enduring than any altar.

The poet and the poet alone has the words in which high emotion perfectly discovers and expresses itself, the far horizons of faith and vision become the homeland of the soul. No wonder then that the earliest and much of the greatest religious literature has been poetry. This does not make it unreal; it makes it nobly free and true. Religion has suffered more from the preacher who has made an infallible text of the poet's singing line, and the theologian who has made a rigid system of the rapture of the poet's spirit, than it has ever suffered from the lyric flight of the poet's imagination and his report of what he found, sung down out of the blue.

The ethnic religions have always depended more upon the teacher than the preacher; there is no need here to enlarge upon the place of teaching in religion. There is no need either to speak of the centrality of ritual in religion. Ritual always uses words but it uses symbols also and used them before it used words. Ritual creates, alongside the offices of the poet and the teacher, the office of the priest. The preacher is actually the latest comer in any religion. The poet sang to what gods he knew, the priest served their altars, the teacher instructed their worshipers, but the prophet spoke for them. He made God's will articulate in flaming words of rebuke and command, and offered for proof of their divine inspiration only their truth and power.

Great-hearted Bishop Charles H. Williams called Christian preaching the creation of the Hebrew prophet and the Greek rhetorician. It is exactly that—with the magic of the spoken word in primitive shadows far and faint behind prophet and rhetorician. The preacher has been propagandist and apologist; theologican and educator; comforter and inspirer; interpreter and authority; echo and rubber stamp; defender of lost causes and pioneer of impossible loyalties; conformist of the conformers and herald of new dawns. He has never in the essential empowerment of his vocation ceased to be a prophet. He has said: "Thus saith the church," "the creeds," "the Bible," or "the schools," but whenever he reached some lonely light-touched height on the ultimate frontier of the Godward side of life he has said: "Thus saith the Lord!" His power is to stand there alone; his gift is to hear and report some authentic word of God.

V.

Something of this has been common to all religion, "one accent of the Holy Ghost the heedless world hath never lost." The augur, the priestess at Delphi, Zoroaster in the Persian mountains, and Gautama under the Bo-tree have all in their own fashions claimed a divine illumination, but at their best they have had little in common with the spirit and content of Hebrew prophecy. In the misty backgrounds of it are wandering bands of religious enthusiasts, dervishes of a Hebrew cast, with their own "schools." They were soothsayers a little, agitators a good deal, patriots after their fashion, and always a positive influence in a slowly developing religion. They show dimly through the Hebrew Old Testament but, since they wrote nothing, little record of what they said is left and not much of what they did.

Then, and almost without ancestry, the great succession begins—Amos, Micah, Isaiah, sons of their time and their race, dating an epoch in religion. For their race believed that a man may be so God-inspired that his message is the articulation of the divine—the voice of religious authority charged with ethical passion. They claimed no ordained succession. "I am no prophet," said Amos, "nor am I a member of a prophetic order . . . the Lord took me . . . and the Lord said to me, go. When the lion roars who does not fear? When the Lord speaks, who will not prophesy?"

They were men who lived apart, nurtured in desert loneliness, or else they were lonely in a king's palace. They spoke always out of strange brooding. They possessed a spiritual sensitiveness which objectified the strongly felt, and had courage and certainty to say: "The Lord took me . . . and the Lord said to me." Thus inspired, the prophet had of necessity an unstudied gift of noble eloquence and a power to make song of a vision; so he moved the world.

He disappeared presently, not all at once but slowly and in a fog of symbolism.* His last phase was like a sunset of mingled gloom and glory in which the clouds take strange shapes, plastic to the imagination, with an allure for minds which love to find forms in the clouds and quarrel and argue about them as though it mattered. What he did at his best shaped the faith of three great religions; what he wrote created a sacred literature. He left the world a faith, a passion, and kindling records of what he did and said. The priest—for whom he had no love—supplanted him with altar rituals. The psalmist continued his music more gently, making it mostly a religion of personal piety, whereas the prophet in his noblest phase stood for a religion of social justice. Then the preacher took his writings for comment or searched them for a text.

Prophecy was thus in its last Hebrew phase "stepped down" to preaching. The synagogue furnished the setting; the sacred Roll supplied the passage for translation into the vernacular, exposition, and comment. Learning and some natural gift seem to have been the only requisites for the office of reader and expounder, though in general the rabbis were a class apart. Teaching and preaching were closely interwoven, but whereas Micah said: "Thus saith the Lord," the Rabbi said: "Thus saith the Roll." Jesus Himself would take a Sabbath service and give to the lesson for the day an application to His own authority which summoned His hearers to discipleship or stung them to wrath. The group about Him were trained in the same tradition. When they accepted His mandate and began to

---

* Symbolism, some maintain, attends the decadence of art and religion, the sign of something greater gone. This is worth thinking through.

press Him and His claims and cause upon the world, they had no choice or resource save to preach. So Christian preaching began.

VI.

It inherited the Old Testament, the tradition of synagogue worship, and the Way, the Truth, and the Life of Jesus. It had as yet no sacred literature of its own, nor anything at all save its faith, its passion, and its hope. It was the first resource of a church which was not yet the Church and a gospel which was not yet the Gospel. The New Testament, in Acts and the Epistles, distinguishes between apostolic preaching which was authoritative and a preaching which claimed to be prompted by the Holy Spirit but was dangerously subjective. The "prophet" of Paul's letters—whose enthusiasm he somewhat distrusted—is wandering, highly individualistic, unordained. It is likely that he contributed indirectly to the growing centralization of church authority through some need of having a recognized authority to hold him in check. Presently he fades out of the picture though his spiritual descendants have persisted. Once the church had its own authoritative literature— the New as well as the Old Testament—preaching took the line it has since followed. This demanded trained men, and the first theological college was founded in Alexandria. It naturally had a chair of homiletics with such occupants as Clement and Origen, who would adorn any faculty.

Christian preaching inherited also a habit of the pagan world whose influence upon it has not often been recognized. The wandering Christian "prophet" finding his audience where he could and saying what he was moved to say was only another species in the Græco-Roman world of a most familiar genus. The empire seems to have been as full of earnest-minded individuals "telling the world" from the classic equivalent of a soap box, as Hyde Park on a Sunday afternoon. There was no press, free or otherwise; no way, save by the spoken word, of creating public opinion, broadcasting news, or advocating a cause. Here was a very great civilization and an empire responsible for the administration of the entire basin of the Mediterranean in which books were the luxury of the rich and newspapers were unknown. (A fascinating book is waiting to be written on historic substitutes for printer's ink.)

The itinerant rhetorician or enthusiast was thus in the Græco-Roman world the substitute for all our agents of publicity and agitation. "Speech," says Martha,* "was free provided it was not seditious, and the first-come orator could harangue the crowd." Martha's chapter on *"La Prédication Morale Populaire"* is a most engaging study of moral idealism in the last phase of the empire, of popular propaganda and the dominance of the "orator" in the milieu out of which Christian preaching emerged. Little enough of this is reflected in early Christian literature.

The writings of St. Paul and his school date from a period in which the morals of the empire supplied a clinical material for the doctrine of human depravity ample enough for even the most despairing. If there were a better side, as there must have been (for a society so rotten as many passages in the Epistles suggest could not have held together), it did not suit the doctrinal ends of the apostle to the Gentiles to recognize it. The separatist element in Christianity was already in action, and abysmal alienations between the church and the "world" were taking a form pregnant with tragic consequences for both the church and the world. Perhaps if Christianity had been kinder to the pagan world—or even more just—the pagan world would have been kinder or more just to Christianity.

* *Les Moralistes Sous L'Empire Romain*, Librairie Hachette et Cie, Paris, 1907, page 215.

There was actually in the second and third Christian centuries the emergence of what Martha calls "a profound and delicate moral idealism." As the empire grew old it grew both wise and sad, and, like men who grow old sadly, haunted by the memories of a careless youth and a maturity spent in the misuse of power, it began to take account of its soul. How far this issued out of vast and inevitable movements of history, how far it reflected indirectly some influence of Christian idealism, how far it was the conscious effort of a society already sensible of approaching doom to save itself is now beyond our power to recover and decide. We only know that, as the long day of Rome drew to its sunset and dark, a bright and even tender light shone through the gathering clouds—and shone too late.

This "profound and delicate" morality was the creation of the Stoic philosophers and has found its classic expression in Marcus Aurelius's examination of his conscience. What was best in ancient Rome took to it kindly because its austere note was native to the Roman spirit. The mixed population of the empire took to it far less kindly. It was too high and hard for them. They sought instead the enticing initiations, the mystic exaltations, and the assured salvations of the mystery religions, and while the emperor meditated upon the meanings of life and duty, his soldiers prayed to Mithras and bowed their bare heads and backs to a bath of bull's blood to wash away their sins.

VII.

Thus all the elements which the church was to take over and recast and redirect were already there; religious address and ritual, propaganda, edification, and longing for salvation. Many of the elements which have been continued in Christian preaching were already there also. First and most creative was the popularization of morality with a philosophical basis.

Preaching with a philosophic basis is never likely to be popular but there is a good deal to be said for it notwithstanding. Philosophy, says Martha again, is the last guardian of reason and dignity in an old and decadent society. It outlives laws, institutions, and morals. No force can prohibit it, no tyranny enslave it, for it is able to find refuge in the invisible searching of an honest heart. Unhappy times revive its force, and the degradation of character only kindles it with a more generous ardor. But it needs much "stepping down" before it can reach and move the generality, and even then it brings with it some breath of coldness native to the heights from which it descends. It must be made near and warm and alive. This became the task of the pagan preacher; he did it with a passion and power from which the less cultured Christian preacher learned much.

It would be rewarding to compare Dion Chrysostom (pagan preaching had also its golden-mouthed ones), whom Martha offers as most representative of these evangelists of the good life, with St. Paul or Bossuet. Dion, like Bossuet, preached in an emperor's palace and to the emperor; Paul got no further than the imperial slaves. Dion could have been called preacher in ordinary to Trajan and he seems on the whole to have had more influence over the Antonine than Bossuet had over the Bourbon. He suffered like St. Paul at the hands of the stormy populace of Greece and Asia Minor.

Dion preached out of the austere Stoic philosophy, St. Paul out of a life "hid with Christ in God." Dion had an ethic; St. Paul had a gospel which was the profound distinction between Stoic and Christian preaching. Nevertheless, Martha thinks, Dion and his fellow-workers prepared the soil for the Christian preacher. They kept alive the right and tradition of free public speech. They had a concern for noble and effective address, they accustomed even the mob to some thought about the serious things of life, and "in expounding morals they prepared the multitude to understand the homilies." "These usages of public discourse, this right of the first-come to take the word in the circus, the theatres, and the assemblies, this right even to speak to the people harshly about themselves, permitted the early Christians to exhort the people without astonishing them." They might be hissed and abused but they were heard. "If the hearts were as yet shut against the new religion, the ears were open."

The philosophical moralist was one thing, the rhetorician was another. He was the humanist of his time who made an art of oratory when letters fell into decay. He lived in a world where there was much to correct and more to mourn. Held in restraint by the Roman administration, the rhetorician —generally Greek—had no domain but the long past and his ingenious imagination. He fought the Persian wars again, grew tearful over Menelaus when Helen left his bed and board. It is always safe to praise, and he praised emperors who deserved no praise, the city which entertained him, his audience, and things of no consequence at all. It was all a game which brought recognition, money, and applause, but he taught Christian preachers their rhetoric.

The applause, Martha says, echoed even in Christian temples. John Chrysostom both protested and, being human, enjoyed it. Augustine, who was severe enough with himself and human nature, tolerated it, though whether it was a tribute to his skill or only another evidence of the fallen estate of human nature may have perplexed the saint in his meditation. What matters is that the art of public address had never been so cultivated in every detail of it—voice, gesture, adroitness—as in the period out of which Christian preaching emerges in full force. The taste for ample and highly rhetorical speech was universal. Preaching, of course, took advantage of this interest and continued the art. Augustine had been teacher of rhetoric, John Chrysostom was trained by a master rhetorician. Pagan rhetoricians would, after their conversion, certainly consecrate their art to the church. The chance to use this old art in a new field may have aided conversion.

VIII.

By the fourth century, then, all the elements which made preaching possible both as an art and a religious force were in action. The church was at last free to come out of the shadows of fear and persecution, to build, organize, and appeal. Its sacred books were assembled and invested with final authority, its organization was effective, its doctrines were beginning to take creedal form, its persuasion of imperial destiny was sure. The gods and goddesses of Olympus had long been dethroned; they were only ghosts haunting the twilight of pagan faith. The final engagement of Christianity and the old Roman state religion had taken place about the altar of victory in the Senate Hall at Rome. The Statue of Victory—itself a spoil of war against the Greeks—and the altar beneath it were more than time-worn stone. They were symbols of the pride and power of the empire. There, since Augustus, the Senate had vowed allegiance, burned its incense and offered its Senatorial equivalents of prayer for the safety of the empire and the prosperity of the state.

Symmachus in defending the cult of the altar was the voice of a thousand years, eloquent, sincere, and pathetic: "It seems to me," he said, "that Rome is before you, saying: 'Respect my age and sacred laws, leave me my ancient solemnities, I have so little left—and I am too old to change.'" Ambrose spoke for his faith and the future. His speech was less noble but the altar and the statue were already doomed. The Christian pulpit became the forum of the empire, and the altar of the Eucharist banished all other altars.

Since then preaching in its full-voiced form has been an indispensable aspect of the growth and administration of Christianity. The history of it belongs to the specialist. The mortal wound the Greek church took from Mohammedanism ended and gave no hope of recovery to the great age of Eastern preaching. The darkness into which western Europe fell carried preaching with it, though preaching was the spearhead of the missionary extension of the church from the sixth to the tenth centuries. Preaching is always an esoteric exercise unless it be done in a language people understand. When Latin was dead and the new languages not yet born, it was sure to have been in a hard way. Specialists debate the extent of vernacular preaching during the dark ages; very likely the missionary did the best he could with folk-speech. Cloister preaching was in Latin and probably church preaching also, which would have made it mostly an affair for the chancel. The transepts and naves probably did not greatly care, they had before them the august drama of the mass.*

Preaching was reborn in the bright centuries of medievalism. It reached the secular world through the preaching orders, became lyric with St. Francis, safeguarded orthodoxy with the Dominicans, and began to sow the seeds of a strange unrest with the Lollards. The prophet reappeared among the Friends of God and the Brethren of the Common Life. Out of all this ferment the Reformation issued, and, with an instinctive necessity, seized upon preaching as its weapon and sacrament. The lights upon the altar were put out, the altar disappeared, the drama of the mass was banished. The pulpit and the Book took the place of the altar. Nothing was left but the preacher and his voice. Once again the Word became God.

In such ways as these the history of changing minds and

* For a solid and very inclusive history of preaching, see Dargan, A. C., Armstrong & Son, New York, 1906. It is packed with facts and names.

times, the emergence of new religious forces, the drama of the soul, and the realities of religion have been reflected in preaching. It has been an epitome of the religious history of the Western world without which that history would have to be rewritten with no possible knowledge of how to write it. The course of it across the centuries can be traced in an unbroken succession of men who made a throne of the pulpit. It has chosen its succession where it would.

Bernard was nobly born, Luther was the son of a Saxon stone mason, Newman's father was a banker, Alexander Whyte's mother an unmarried Scotch peasant, John Wesley was born in an English rectory, St. Francis was a medieval merchant's son, Dwight Moody spent his boyhood on a bare New England farm. The allure of it has called to the ministry unfailing generations of ardent youth who have found in preaching to handfuls of folk in obscure stations the fascinating exercise of a vocation whose perfection is always beyond them and whose spell they can neither escape nor explain. Yet always it has been a strange vocation, a man's voice proclaiming God's will, a man's word enshrining God's Word.

The genius of it, like the wind, bloweth where it listeth. No school can create it, no analysis quite explain it. Its commerce is with the unseen, its authority in the insight of the preacher's mind and the strangely quickened passion of his spirit. Its history has been romance and dusty mediocrity. It has been flame and ashes but its fire has never gone out. And now when preaching never seemed more secure or brilliantly served, there begins to fall across it for the first time in its history a disturbing shadow. It has to take account, as everything else, of a changing world which does not know where it is going and a confused mind which can do no more than question and wait.

CHAPTER II

PREACHING UNDER FIRE

FOR most Protestants, "going to church" and listening to a sermon are much the same thing. The movements under way in evangelical churches to recover the primacy of worship and make it an entirely adequate religious vehicle are not yet generally so advanced as to reduce the sermon to a liturgical incident. Actually poor preaching and bare worship usually go together. When they do they make a dismal combination in face of which church attendance is kept up by habit, by the longing of lonely folk for fellowship, and by loyalty to the church as a sacred institution with which are associated the "means of grace."

Very likely this last association has carried institutional Christianity across the ages and carries it still with little regard to the quality of preaching. Religion is associative in the very nature of it. The altar, the priest, or the prophet have always supplied the centers around which it has lived. When these have lost their power to assemble, support, or inspire the seekers after God, religion itself begins to be undone. Few enough seekers after God in the long succession of the devout have been strong enough to make their pilgrimage without a comrade. When Christian had seen Faithful "carried up through the clouds with sound of trumpet, the nearest way to the Celestial Gate," he was lonely enough till Hopeful joined him. Most Christians need a considerable company of Faithfuls and

Hopefuls if they are to get bravely on toward the Celestial City.

Loyalty to the church as an institution without which our common life would be impoverished and endangered is, very likely, the second major support of attendance. This loyalty to what Royce called "the beloved community" gets fused in indefinable ways with the reality of religion on one side and supplies on the other side an opportunity for the expression of loyalty in action so characteristic of the time. I had the good fortune once to be associated with a group of young men and women whose devotion to their church and minister constitutes a moving memory. The men were all of a type; engineers, salesmen, and executives of the select and forceful sort which the city of Detroit, at the peak of its great industrial activity, called and trained. I never asked of them a service or even a sacrifice for their church to which they did not eagerly respond. One had only to indicate anything which could be done or organized and then forget it. When the time came it was there arranged to the last detail. And they came to church regularly.

Yet, whether it was my own fault, their limitation, or a subtle aspect of something which had caught and characterized us all, I did not know then nor do I know now what religion as an experience meant to them, nor what mind they had about their inherited religion. I do not think they knew themselves. They could dissect and rebuild an internal combustion engine or solve triumphantly the most intricate engineering problems, but the deep rootings and functioning of their own vigorous personalities were beyond them. Nor had they any words to uncover the drama of their souls. And after all what was the drama of the soul compared with the proud drama of a city whose new towers were reflected in an old river, whose prosperity was intoxicating, whose creations were filling the roads

of a continent. The last new model of a car was drama enough
for them.

I.

Preaching was—and is—crucial in this confused situation. It
did not carry, never has carried, the whole weight of any
church, but the power and quality of it have made the difference between a strongly going church and a limping church.
A church would keep going under unappealing preaching but
always with falling attendance and difficult finance. (Attendance and finance have been—and are—the official tests of a
successful ministry.) Of course, ministerial executive ability
counted strongly.

Our larger churches had become very complicated and demanding organizations. Their ministers did not always need
to be golden-mouthed. If they were strong-willed, ingenious,
resourceful, deft in their human touch, they often did very
nicely. But on the whole their preaching carried them and
their churches. What I am trying to say is this: American
church life has been a "complex" carried by many forces with
preaching at the center. Preaching made religion articulate;
the church made it concrete.

The layman had little choice in his acceptances or rejections.
He took it all or left it all. He might and often did find fault
with his minister. He has not been inclined to pay much
attention to preaching as help or handicap to religion generally.
He knows that he does not have to listen to it if he does not
want to. If he is leaving the church out of his life, it is not
because he objects to preaching in itself but because religion
has become for him a confused matter whose definite bearing
upon his own well-being he neither sees clearly nor feels deeply.

It is impossible to document these conclusions; they are rather
the result of observation than the record of definite statements.

I have taken some pains to find out the attitude of thoughtful and high-idealed young people who are leaving the church out of their lives. What they say comes at bottom to this: They can, they believe, live happily and usefully without it. They find their motivations in another region—and also their values. The disturbing recognition of this trend is probably responsible for the preacher's growing concern for his own vocation. He sees the full and careless tides which run past his church doors and asks why. It is to his credit that he begins with himself. His disquiet is significant; when craftsmen doubt the validity of their own craft, something is gone.

He approaches the present estate of organized Christianity through his own congregation, and unless he be fortunate in force and station, what he sees is not assuring. Empty pews are voiceless, but they are disconcertingly concrete witnesses to something. No wonder he sees them as a judgment upon the effectiveness of his own ministry. If he does not, his official board will very likely call them to his attention. These general statements are subject to qualification. Statistically the churches are holding their own and a little more. Where parochial conditions have been stable, church attendance seems to have maintained itself with no great change. Population trends, the decay of rural life, the fluidity of residential areas in rapidly growing cities—all have to be taken in account. It has been said, though I cannot "document" it, that there are between two and three "sittings" in the total number of Protestant churches for the total number of members.* William Warren Sweet's *The Story of Religions in America* (or the author's *Religion in Our Times*) examines the forces which have produced this condition. At any rate this present ministerial generation has inherited a costly and disheartening

* In Catholic churches, on the contrary, about three communicants for each sitting.

amount of empty (and unfillable) church space. The attempt to fill it has been responsible for a good deal of the misdirection of misdirected preaching.

The Protestant ministry (I can speak for no other) are almost pathetically eager for any light upon their task, any help to do it better. The popular criticism of the ministry is unjust. No one thing can be said about them unqualifiedly. They are quite human and as various in type as their congregations but they are devoted to their work, often living sacrificial lives, eager for the Realm of God. Their moral and social vision is generally in advance, as it should be, of their congregations. If they are using outmoded instruments they are willing to change them— more willing often than their congregations. The numbing inertias of Protestant Christianity are not in the pulpit; they are in the pews—even when the pews are empty. The pulpit is, therefore, just now examining its status, its assets and liabilities as never before. Preaching both in detail and as the method of the churches is crucially involved in these revaluations. I shall consider toward the end of this chapter the attitude of critical religious educators toward preaching, and begin here with a movement in Protestantism which is certainly supplementing preaching and, in its most fully developed forms, radically changing its status.

II.

It is now a hundred years since Keble's famous Assize sermon—a rather dull sermon to have done so much—began a movement which has not so much dethroned the sermon as edged it out of the spotlight. This phrase is neither so irreverent nor irrelevant as it sounds. In all evangelical churches which have now come strongly under the influence of the Oxford movement the highlights fall, quite literally, not upon the pulpit but upon the communion table, which has taken on far more than the emergent outlines of an altar. The pulpit is no longer central in architecture, liturgy, or the ideology of worship. Worship and not preaching, say the spokesmen of this movement, carries the content and reality of religion. No other foundation is broad enough or constant enough.

Religion, they say, began in ritual and liturgy. These are older than any words about them. The word-structure, the "myth," * was developed to explain and defend them, grew up around the altar. The altar, its sacrifices and sacraments can be explained, interpreted, garmentured by words and defended by reason, but they are rooted in something deeper than reason and older than any words. The recentering of religion around the altar will, they maintain, furnish it its own true and strong foundation and incidentally save public worship from being balanced upon the devoted head of the preacher with some precarious support from a "quartet"—which is very much like standing a pyramid upon its apex. It can be done but it demands a deal of shoring up.

There is another side to this whole contention; there is certainly an "escape" element in it. Acute critics of the movement see a great danger in this subordination of the prophet to the priest. The priest, they say, is not only a servant of tradition, concerned with patterned forms, but his vision, focused upon his altar and shut in by temple walls, tends to miss the welter of the outer world. His lights come transfigured through windows which shut out the actinic truth and fact rays. His excessive dependence upon symbols may actually be due to the lack of a strong intellectual hold upon religious reality. His social vision is dim, his social passion subordinate to the interests of his church and his orders. Such critics have a disconcerting amount of testimony from the general history of re-

---

* Used in quite the literal sense of the word.

ligion and the history of the Christian church at their command, and they use it tellingly.

The first leaders of the Oxford movement were strangely insensitive to abuses in Anglicanism whose attempted correction by the state kindled whatever fire there was in Keble's Assize sermon. The church, they held, having an authority above and beyond and sacerdotally apart from the authority of the state, should be left to cleanse its own temple. But they themselves made little effort toward that much-needed process and used their whip of small cords mostly upon fellow-Christians who disagreed with them. They were equally insensitive to the grave social and economic wrongs of their time.

It is only fair to say that Anglo-Catholicism has now a noble social passion. Its leaders are among our most intelligent and effective seekers for social righteousness and have furnished an illuminating approach to a Christian use of the world in their sacramental conceptions of life. Nevertheless, their critics have a case though the movement against which they protest goes on. It has slowly created in the evangelical churches a new and entirely defensible concern for worship, and the quest for forms of church service in which the sermon inevitably takes a diminished or even secondary place.

Churches in which preaching thus became secondary to liturgical worship and sacramentarianism, it is now held, command the support and devotion of their communicants as the pulpit-focused sanctuaries cannot do. I doubt if the facts bear this out. The Anglican and Lutheran churches, cited as enviable examples of what Protestant worship should be, have great corporate solidity but they doubtless feel the stress of the time. At any rate the whole liturgical and sacramental movement furnishes an alternative with which preaching has to reckon.

It has also—this is a shop-worn commonplace—to reckon with

any amount of competition. The catalogue of competitors writes itself—many of them old foes with new faces. I can remember easily enough a New England June or October Sunday morning when the family horse and surrey sadly depleted the "stated services" of the sanctuary. It seems now a rather blameless worldiness and when I contrast, in retrospect, the sermons these "worshipers of nature" missed, with the allure of now vanished roads which followed birch and hemlock-shaded softly singing brooks back to their sources in enchanted hills, I have no quarrel with my sometime errant parishioners. If they and the roads and the high-bred horses could come to life again together, I would desert any church to be their comrade for a blue and gold Sunday morning.

Those vanished roads are symbols of many other vanished things: a steadfast social order, patterned morality, the unchallenged priority of evangelical Protestantism, Sundays kept reasonably free from commercialized amusement, relative simplicities of life and interest. Perhaps something far more difficult to put into words is also gone: a quiet and well ordered security, a unity of steadfast happiness which had not as yet felt the dissolving touch of forces even then nearer the thresholds of the church than we dreamed. All these vanished things sustained the churches. Their dissolution has deeply affected every phase of church life and involved preaching in the general confusion of the time.

Whether the radio is or will become a telling competitor of face-to-face preaching is uncertain. The preachers who have the privilege of the air certainly solidify their own positions and extend their fame. There is no way of knowing how far they keep the devout away from church, create among the undevout an effective interest in religion, or really meet the needs of the religious. Variously assorted wave-lengths in the latest scientific equivalent of the ether would seem to be slight chains to bind the listener to the throne of God, especially when they can be broken by a turn of the wrist. The expectation of the more ingenious that all preaching will presently be done over a nation-wide hook-up by a few homiletic sovereigns of the air seems premature. If preaching ever loses the support of personal affection fostered by pastoral care and the human touch, it is doubtful if it can be carried by what engineers—who always have a sound concern for foundations—call sky-hooks.

Preaching has to reckon with current religious literature. The publication of religious books—or books about religion—has been for a generation now an extensive business. It has commanded highly resourceful editors who have been generous in their definitions of religion and tireless in pursuit of titles. They do not themselves know accurately who, besides preachers and religious educators, read their publications. Probably not many —relatively. Any number of published sermons are included— but these do not keep the generality from church.

In a heightened way the function which preaching has hitherto exercised is now distributed among religious educators, moralists, dramatists, and novelists, but these should be as much contributors to the preacher's message as competitors of his art. They supply him advertisable topics and matter for comment. In fact, a good deal of popular preaching takes advantage of the interest which they create and floats its craft on their tides. Preaching should find in all this some substance and little competition.

Thoughtful essayists have always contributed interpretations of life and its issues which, at their best in form, content, and insight, challenge any sermon and have besides a free, ranging quality few sermons possess; but they are read only by the elect and rarely pay for publication. They are contributions to insight and continue one of the noblest traditions of letters. They

have little bearing upon the status of preaching save to supply
the preacher models of style, a vital subject matter of which he
does not always avail himself; and reproach him for the inepti-
tude of his pen. It is doubtless true, however, that the distrac-
tion of intellectual interest through the superabundance of
printed matter has affected popular interest in sermons unfavorably. The pulpit has, or should have, a region particularly its own, but it has lost its monopoly.

III.

The most acute critics of preaching as a vehicle for ethics
and religion take another line. They are not concerned with
the argument between preaching and liturgy. The printing
press, they recognize, has changed the status of preaching—
that is as may be. Preaching, they contend, no longer serves
the true interest of religious thought and moral and social
quest; it is essentially propaganda, blameless and well inten-
tioned propaganda, but still propaganda.

They may beg the question by the use of that malodorous
word, but they have a case. Preaching by the nature of it
assumes authority—"Thus saith the Lord," "Thus saith the
creeds," "Thus saith the Bible, the church, hallowed tradition,
inherited faith, hallowed habit." If the preacher neither quotes
nor assumes any of these authorities—which he commonly does
—he cannot escape, if his preaching is to be effective, a more
subtle assumption of authority—"Thus saith the preacher."

Preachers whose sermons are quests rather than pronounce-
ments, who think aloud their inquiring way through perplexities to no triumphant issue, may secure and serve a sympathetic and understanding following but they will preach to
many vacant pews. Preaching may challenge the outworn with
a new dogmatism—Chrysostom and Augustine, the Reformers
and Wesleys did that. It may militantly defend an established

order against doubters and rebels—Bernard of Clairvaux did that. It may interpret and embroider the accepted, extend the frontiers of the familiar into unexplored regions—all great preachers have done that. It may launch crusades, it may herald, amid the shadows, the sure rising of dawns whose anticipated glory has already flooded the preacher's soul—the prophets did that. It may seem to argue when its conclusions are already predetermined—all preachers do that.

But it cannot patiently accumulate facts, examine and weigh them, submit them to merciless cross-examination and be willing to be led by them no matter where they go, and still remain preaching. Its movement will be slowed, its passion cooled, its glory gone. Now, say these critics, this patient, undogmatic process of inquiry, necessarily slow and as yet greatly confused, is exactly what religion and its related interests need more than anything else. It cannot, they contend, escape it. The time may come when the preacher may enter into his own again with a re-established gospel of sovereign certainties.

Just now the thoughtful must take another line. These critics do not tell us what they themselves would substitute; they are at present experimenting with the "group" technique. Preaching, as far as they are concerned, may take its time about dying. But its roots, they say, are cut. Preaching is also, they urge, handicapped because it loves the dramatic and tends so to dramatize any situation as to get it out of drawing. Also it loves to go crusading, and if no crusade is in sight goes out of its way to start one. Our own time, they hold, is suffering already from an excess of murky drama and tired of crusades which have captured and held no holy city.

All this cannot be "non-suited." There is always a necessary stage in religious and social inquiry, never more acutely insistent than now, for which preaching is no vehicle. Our entire church life may be so excessively institutionalized, so entangled in this present world to which it has given too many hostages, as to make it difficult or impossible for Christianity, as now organized, to recover its lost radiance or recapture and creatively express the vision of Jesus and make His spirit dominant. I do not think this is entirely true; it is dangerously near being true. The slow dissolution of the Christian enterprise into like-minded groups with no loyalty save to the Way, the Truth, and the Life of Jesus Christ might mean the rebirth of Christianity. If that would happen it would carry inherited preaching with it. Something like this may be written on the unturned pages of history. No one knows.

But here and now the group-and-inquiry technique leaves the religious needs of most folk unmet. If one accepts the contentions of this critical group at their face value, the results of patient inquiry and the sifted remnant of discussion must still, if they are to have meaning and value for the generality of religious people, be mediated to them with passion and authority. I doubt if it would be possible to substitute the "group" method for the now going concern of the churches for any considerable length of time without either creating new forms of institutional religion strangely like the old, or making of religion itself an errant ghost. It must be kept going in corporate forms—if it has any right to be kept going at all. Preaching is still a vital vehicle for that—or might be made its vital vehicle. Actually I do not believe the strain which preaching now acknowledges is due centrally to any one of these forces, competitive or critical. They all count, but they are only aspects of a situation which meets us on a wider front.

IV.

We have already considered the preacher's inheritance, though not all of it. He is the heir of the prophet and the rhetorician. His vocation has been shaped, colored, given content, what you will, by the vast and many-branched growth of the Christian mind and the Christian church. He has inherited creeds, loyalties, authorities, hopes, and confidences. His inheritances are as old as the first dim commerce of our puzzled humanity with the mystery of the world without and the loneliness of its own spirit. Yesterday they seemed entire and sure; the fabric of his faith woven and rewoven across the centuries was bright, strong, unraveled. Then in one long generation it began to be questioned and undone.

A new mind began to emerge—a new mind about the facts and forces of the physical world; about human origins and history; about human nature and personality; about the sources and documents of the Bible; about the source-facts of Christianity and about religion itself. As far as this mind is still religious, it faces far-reaching readjustments. If it is not interested in religion, it is able for the first time in history to find a unified system of thought, motivation, and satisfaction and leave religion—as it has always been defined and practiced—out of account.

What one might call middle-level preaching has always depended upon the accepted doctrinal social and ethical structure of inherited Christianity. It has been a good deal like inheriting a skyscraper whose foundations had long been laid, whose steel construction was already in place. What could or could not be done was already determined by the very nature of the framework. The figure is elusive but in substance rather right. Theological training built the structure of Christian faith into the minds of successive generations of preachers, furnished them with a doctrinal articulation, indicated their authorities, drilled them in texts, stored their minds with useful homiletical material, and dismissed them hopefully.

They were then examined by denominational authorities for possible deviations from the faith and practice of their communions. If the theological schools had done their work well, alarming deviations were rare; especially if the candidates had been skilfully instructed in such formulæ as ease or conceal the strain between changing minds and rigid creeds. The congregations to whom those thus trained and vouched for preached had themselves been nurtured in the same system. The more religiously intelligent knew what the preacher was going to say as soon as he announced his text. Guardians of orthodoxy were quick to detect sins of doctrinal omission and commission. Sermons began, continued, and ended within the beams and girders and upon the foundations of this hallowed order.

Preachers Sunday after Sunday laid its beams anew, explored its foundations to show how deep and strong they were, called the unsheltered to take refuge within it—the one unshaken and unshakable shelter—

> "How rise thy towers, serene and bright
> To meet the dawning day!
> In vain the surges angry shock,
> In vain the drifting sands;
> Unharmed upon the eternal rock
> The Eternal City stands."

From the upper levels of this structure of faith they displayed its encompassing horizons of hope and pointed to a road out of all shadow and storm to the timeless peace of heaven. It was—and is—a spacious structure with room enough in it for faith and dreams and duties and whatever our perturbed humanity needs of comfort and assurance. Preachers as long as they kept within it have never needed to feel cramped. For the most part they had no desire to leave it and, if they had, they would not have known where to go.

Those of them for whom it is no longer a shelter are more perplexed by their theological homelessness than exultant in their freedom. I am writing now of evangelical Protestantism and its major denominations. The liberal churches gave their ministers a less exacting examination to begin with and more freedom of experimentation to go on with. Their doctrinal structures have tended to become rather mellow ruins, but in some shadowy fashion the old foundations held and the old controls also. For the most part preaching began with the same assumptions and ended with unexpectedly similar conclusions or exhortations.

There was always, then, something for a preacher to say. He had a system of doctrine to set forth, a Book to expound and a strongly established belief about the duties, relationships, and issues of life with which to meet and explain recurrent experiences or new elements of crisis or challenge. He passed all this through what he was himself, and its uniformity therefore was variously mediated. Preachers of imagination, insight, poetic faculty, and resource in the fresh handling of old themes were able to touch their work with really high distinction. They found fascinating roads from time-worn texts to regions of vision and inspiration. They extended the implications of Christianity and dealt penetratingly with individual and social needs. The medieval mind found many symbols in the architecture and furnishings of its cathedrals. The towers were, they sometimes said, the bishops and high churchmen. Great preachers have always been the towers of the Protestant churches, but the structure of their faith and doctrine held them up.

V.

This structure of faith and doctrine gave content to preaching. The vital power of it has very likely lain in another and not often explored region—the interpretative faculty of the congregation. The preacher and the congregation must not only speak the same language; they must live in the same world; the same imponderable world of faith, experience, and inheritance. They must share between them a community of understanding which, like the understanding of those who have lived long together, needs few words for the happy commerce of their spirits. Even then what the sermon says means little enough until the congregation gives it meaning through some subtle and sometimes unexpected appropriation and application of their own. It is like weaving one fabric on two looms, if that is possible, and getting a different pattern on the two sides of the same piece of cloth.

What the preacher says links up association paths in the hearer's mind, and the hearer is then off on some excursion of his own—profitable or unprofitable—the course and conclusion of which would often startle the preacher who started it. Also, and this is more to the point, the preacher is always dependent upon the congregation for the interpretation of what he says in terms of life experience. The great phrases of mystic and evangelical religion have always depended for their carrying power upon the experiences of the congregation. It was never easy to explain "saved by grace" or "cleansed in the blood of the Lamb," but those who had brought the travail of their divided souls to the altar rail and risen reborn and praising God knew by a knowledge beyond words to say.

It is equally difficult to define "hid with Christ in God," "the God-filled life," "the Christ-filled life," nor is it easy to explain the more mystical doctrinal phrases such as "living bread," or the "water of life." Glowing and creative phases of Christian thought and experience have in these words and phrases been reduced almost to symbols and passed from generation to generation. The more evangelically minded among our students find it almost impossible to begin, continue, or end a sermon without using some of them. They reflect a patterned preaching whose power in the past no one would deny, nor whose significance for the present, if they are illuminatingly interpreted, no friend of religion will question. We call such phrases—for want of a better name—mystico-theological, and the preaching which is strongly colored by them mystico-theological preaching. Most of the older and best loved hymns use the same phrases, appeal to the same experiences. Prayer is saturated with them.

They begin, maybe to the great loss of religion, to sound remote—though there are always in almost every congregation men and women who find them the "bread of life" and count preaching barren which does not use them. Such as these could never put into any clear words what they understand by them. Their own experiences of piety and prayer, of faith and obedience unlock mystic hidden meanings and give to words which others find meaningless the light and shadow, the passion, action, and triumphant issue of the drama of their souls.

Preaching thus depends and always to an unsuspected degree upon the interpretative contribution of the congregation. Gladstone is said to have defined oratory as giving back in a torrent what the audience supplies in a mist, but here is something more than that. It is often giving in a fog what the hearer changes into light. Effective preaching not only depends upon the power of the hearers to change it, though they cannot explain how, into what sustains and inspires them, it depends also upon some mutual centrality of interest and purpose. I do not think a preacher often really preaches over the heads of his congregation. He does often preach to one side of them, being himself interested in what they do not care for, or thinking of religion in ways in which they do not think of it.

VI.

All this bears at every point upon the difficult estate of preaching today. To begin with, its doctrinal framework is giving way. Even when preaching was not overly theological it assumed a doctrinal support, for after all a Christian preacher must preach the facts and faith of Christianity. Now the facts are all under critical examination and the faith confused. There is no general agreement along the rather embattled Christian front about the conclusions reached, or the objectives to be sought. Considerable sections of the army are engaged in brisk but inconclusive action among themselves. The right and left wings exchange broadsides and, though the casualties are not heavy, morale is unfavorably affected. This, the charitable should recognize, is not so much due to the essentially contentious nature of religious leaders as to their unresolved perplexities. They believe in the supreme significance of their cause; they do not know how to carry it through or toward what ends to direct it.

Church people who have not been consciously affected by the uncertainties and frustrations of the modern religious mind —and these I believe to be the majority in American Protestantism—still feel the strain since there is no perfect insulation against the time-spirit. The more militant harden their own positions excessively in defending them. Controversy becomes more acid because neither side is sure. Something is gone, a deep-poised confidence sustained by the persuasion of an unshaken and unshakable support in the authority and divinely validated veracity of the Christian message.

The critical church historian might maintain that what is thus described as gone never really existed; that church history, like every other history, is the millennial record of tensions, controversies, uncertainties; that the church to which its

founder left the bequest of peace as its most precious inheritance
has never for any long period been inwardly or outwardly entirely at peace. Which is true enough. Strain and reconciliation are the costly steps in the stairs by which we climb—or
down which we fall. But there have been periods of central
certainty and even inner serenity for the Christian enterprise—
bright and all too brief. The last great phase of evangelical
preaching was shaped in a period approximately like that. Now
it is gone for the churches as the equivalent of it is gone for
Western civilization. The steadfast do not admit the fact, but
they cannot escape its implications. The first, the fundamental
perplexity of preaching today is the lack of an authoritative
message for those preachers who share the modern mind and
the lack of an inwardly assured message among those who do
not.

The second perplexing condition of modern preaching is the
gradually diminishing number of men and women who hear
gladly the great key words of the evangelical faith and can,
through some inner grace and faculty of their own, transform
them into a reality and power of religious living. This faculty
of the recipient to make a living reality of the spoken word—
the outer and evident sign of an inner and spiritual grace—
has given to preaching a sacramental character. It may, through
this indefinable transubstantiation, become as really a sacrament
as the broken bread and the cup on the communion table or
at the altar rail. This, and not the wisdom or eloquence of it
is the final secret of its power. And, like the breaking of the
bread and the pouring of the wine, unless the recipient make
it a sacrament, only words and the dying echo of words are left.

The third fundamental perplexity of modern preaching is the
lack of unity in the mind, temper, outlook of any congregation. Not only are the generations side by side in the same

pews, the centuries are there side by side. A cosmology old as Babylon touches elbows with Jeans, Eddington, and Einstein. John Calvin, John Wesley, and Albert Schweitzer meet under the same roof. A piety which believes the Ten Commandments to have been written on tables of stone amid the flame of shaken Sinai worships alongside an intellectual curiosity which traces morals from taboos through customs to accepted conventions and doubts their value for an experimental age—very likely doing some experimenting of its own.

Those for whom religion is entirely a man's relationship with his Maker, personal and subjective, cross the same threshold with those for whom religion is "social idealism become passionate and determined—an inspiring vision of the unrealized possibilities of life." * And it would be strange if there were not in most congregations an appealing remnant for whom religion is only "wishful thinking" always dissolving and always taking form again, who can do no more than "follow the gleam." The natural assembly and fixation of minds and tempers in congenial denominations, the selective power of different types of preaching and worship, go a good way toward securing a working coherence in the average congregation, but even this coherence is giving way before an invasion which cannot for the present be repelled.

What can a preacher do when his vocation is under fire from the friends of religion, his own mind very often troubled and when he takes into the pulpit with him both the confusions and perplexities which it is his sacred vocation to dispel? The blind are not yet leading the blind, but the leader and the led are in the fog together. I would qualify all this as it should be qualified. There are preachers to honor and be glad for, whose mes-

* From a wise and glowing sermon of Dr. Ernest Fremont Tittle delivered October 8, 1933.

sage is nobly constructive, whose vision sees beyond the fog
the sovereign stars.   The hearing they receive and the influence
they exert are a witness that preaching, instead of growing
obsolete, is indispensable if the reality of religion is to be maintained.   But preaching must take account of the times.

CHAPTER III

THE CHANGING PHASES OF
CHRISTIAN PREACHING

A ND the times, for all their seeming coldness to preaching,
are on the preacher's side. Because the mind of the time
is less sure about more things, it is potentially more teachable
and unusually open * to creative suggestion. Because the last
twenty years have been so emotionally disturbing, the need for
emotional stability is extraordinarily acute. Here, if one knew
how to say it, is the master need of the time. We would
better speak of our moods than our minds. Our crucial instability is emotional, our crucial confusions are in our tempers
rather than our convictions. For a generation every agency which
can play upon the major chords of emotion has been brought
into action, and the disintegrating rather than the creative and
unifying emotions have been heightened: fear and not courage;
hate and not good-will; prejudice and not tolerance; the use of
power for aggrandizement and not for the common good.

The mischief of propaganda is what it does to the emotions;
the use and abuse of emotional response for irrational ends.
We have not, through the major agencies acting upon us, been

* Not too open. There are closed minds everywhere and some of
them in highly strategic positions. But the popular mind is open and
the closed mind not so tightly shut. A very representative group of
conservative gentlemen, with whom I lunch weekly, listen occasionally
now without audible explosion to speakers who six years ago would
have given the more plethoric a stroke.

taught to think; we are urged to act through feeling. A time so fashioned is in peril through its emotional plasticity. The post-war period has been ideal for the self-proclaimed Messianic deliverer (who becomes the dictator if he can). We have of late had few makers of Utopias save Mr. Wells whose last Utopia is dated too far in the future to do us any good now, but we have a literature of exploration highly symptomatic. When any voice can get a crowd the preacher might wisely ask why his voice assembles only the faithful. The times are made for him also.

The need for voices wise in interpretation, creative in message, and with a power to substitute a regnant mind for hot moods is desperately insistent. And they must have, if a weltering world is to be saved from itself, the authority of high detachment. The prophet may come out of solitude but he does not come for conference; he comes to announce, "Thus saith the Lord." He has been often enough misled; he has again and again said the living word, but he must be sure the word is alive and he must know how to find it, when to say it and what it is meant to do.

Half the futility of futile preaching is in misdirection. What is said is well enough. Except for rare art in organization and presentation and the gift which elect preachers possess of giving some high quality of interest to their sermons, there is astonishingly little difference in the general substance of Christian preaching. A deal of otherwise good preaching goes wrong because it arrives nowhere.

The French have a word for it, *"echouer,"* which they use technically for ships which run aground. More generally it means to miscarry but always to miscarry as ships do which set out bravely under full sail and end on a reef or a shoal; which is often as true of tall sermons as tall ships though they are more likely to fetch up on a sand-bar than a reef. The drive of most sermons thus misdirected is, however, likely to be so slowed up toward the end that their grounding causes no casualties.

Plenty of sermons with a fairly merchandisable cargo come to little because the congregation neither want nor, maybe, need it, nor in its half hour can be persuaded that they do need it and should want it. Other sermons come to their desired haven with a cargo of edification for the congregation and satisfaction for the preacher through his sure instinct for what then and there ought to be said. This sense of the fitness of the thing said for the time, the situation, and the congregation is one of the most vital gifts for a preacher. I doubt if he has ever been really "called" if he does not possess it.

Here is a matter which goes far beyond the flair of a preacher for a telling topic or the rightness of a sermon for the time and the place. It bears directly upon the relation of preaching generally to the period to which it is addressed. Unless it have a message which an epoch needs, said in a language the epoch understands with some profound correspondence between itself and the time-spirit, its passion will be misspent and its truth—for such preaching may be true—miscarry. It will have power over a period only as its ruling ideas have in them the mastery which the time needs. There is no way the writer knows to bring these rather sapless sentences to life save to illustrate them by some examination of the changing phases of Christian preaching across the centuries.

I.

Preaching takes its force and character from its ruling ideas and its directing purpose, and of these two the ruling ideas are most strategic. Preaching, the books say,* may be doctrinal,

---

* For example, see Coffin's *What to Preach.*

expository, evangelical, educational, † for the edification of the saints and the church, ‡ ethical, apologetic, social. The schools change the names a little but what they mean is much the same. They represent as much the various ends preaching may seek or the forms it may take as the ideas which inform it. They save it from monotony and guide the preacher in his approaches to his congregation. They are more or less standardized forms to keep him from holding to a narrow front. You may call them homiletic fields. Almost every preacher through some deep necessity of temperament is likely to confine his preaching too much to one field and use only one method. If he keep a book like Dr. Coffin's at hand it will help him break his patterns, nobly broaden his conception of preaching, and enrich his program.

But there has been behind these more or less standardized classifications of preaching a vaster movement. Its great epochs of renaissance have been coincident with the discovery and occupation of new regions of faith and duty. Actually this movement from region to region is the conscious or half-unconscious response of the preaching church to the changing spirit and mind of an age. Sometimes the movement is inaugurated by a man or a group of men who see clearly and feel strongly an emergent need while their fellow-preachers, who have not the power in religion Napoleon so coveted in war: "to see what is behind the hill," hold fast to old traditions. Such men, if they have force enough to impose their message upon the lethargic, courage enough to defy the hostile, and words of life and fire, date an epoch in religion, herald a new and luminous dawn. John Wesley and his associates illustrate this perfectly. In such times the preacher rarely comes alone. He is attended by a new choiring of sacred song, by some deep stirring of popular

† Faunce's *The Educational Aspects of the Ministry.*
‡ Jefferson's *Building of the Church.*

emotion, by some widely shared sense of great things ended or begun.

The best illustration of these changing phases of Christian preaching is, of course, just the whole history of it. They have reflected—or voiced—the successive modifications of the Christian mind, the rise or fall of historic orders, and the changing status of the church. Actually the different kinds of preaching were not, to begin with, the creation of the schools. They are what preaching has become when it faced any living situation with a living passion. It was only when the fire had gone out that they became set and hard, to be discussed in a classroom. They were named as so many other things have been named only in retrospect.

The apostles did not learn their technique in any classroom. They would not have known what "apologetic preaching" means. I doubt if they knew that they were "preaching." But when their faith was under fire, their enthusiasm miscalled, and their lives threatened, they flamed out with their defense of their faith and their Lord. When the Jewish church challenged their religion as a departure from its tradition, they interpreted it in terms of ancient prophecy and the expectation of Israel. Because their Master had commanded them to win the world they appealed for fellow-soldiers in His cause. These have been, ever since, the fundamental forms preaching has taken: the defense of its gospel, the interpretation of its faith, the call to Christian discipleship.

None of St. Paul's sermons are reported save as he told more than once the story of his life in defense of himself and his gospel—that and the shortest and most adroit of sermons on Mars Hill. It is very likely, however, that his letters express in a more compact form the substance of his preaching. He developed, therefore, doctrinal preaching and supplied the Christian mind its most considerable body of doctrinal material. He added also another great category—Christian-character-building preaching. He himself calls that very necessary process "the edification of the saints," and the saints needed it sadly enough.

He and his fellow-teachers had to conceive and create in the pagan world a type of character then new to religion and history, shaped by the spirit and injunction of the teaching of Jesus, emancipated at bitter cost from entangling paganism, delivered from low desire and habit, world-denying and world-defying, yet patient, gentle, and asking no weapon for any conflict save its own power to suffer and rejoice. Christianity has no documents, besides the Sermon on the Mount and the parables, so moving and so shining as these final chapters of St. Paul's letters in which he draws with a sure creative touch what a Christian ought to be when Nero was emperor of Rome.

One sees the low rooms on poor streets of cities long gone to dust, lighted by smoking yellow-flamed wicks, where the poor and enslaved were enjoined and challenged to lives of enduring goodness and spiritual glory. There in the shadows a new dawn arose, and their faces were touched with the light of it, a light compared with which Nero's Golden House was dark, a light the mystic apostle called some reflection of the glory of God in the face of Jesus Christ. When they went out again under the stars something went with them which was to change the world.*

II.

Preaching next became the creative instrument of the emerging church for the building of its own structure in a hostile world where, like Nehemiah's workmen, "each of the builders had his sword girded by his side as he built." The church met the power of Rome and the critical drive of

---

* I have already noted, too inadequately, the development of expository preaching. That deserves far more consideration.

Græco-Roman culture through its literature and its preaching. The apologists of patristic Christianity believed, with most great strategists, that attack is the best defense. They challenged the pagan order to meet and match them, point by point, for good-will or goodness, for inner grace, for integrity of faith, nobility of worship, and right to the dominion of the world. Since they had given no hostages to an alien order save their own power to wear it down by suffering and since they backed their words by consistency of life, they won the empire —and lost, in winning it, the unstained weapons by which they had conquered. The habit of challenge-preaching has persisted, but rarely since the third century has the church been in the strategic position which gives all such preaching its final power.

The creedal controversies of the fourth and fifth centuries gave Christian faith and Christian preaching a full doctrinal content of an argumentative turn which has not since essentially changed. The missionary preaching which won for the church the whole of Europe must have been appeal-preaching, though the scanty records which are left would seem to indicate that something besides the preaching of Augustine, Cuthbert, Columba, and Boniface won the cloudy North. We have only one record—and that very lovely—of what brought the followers of Woden and Thor to the cross. Life for them was as a sparrow's flight from wintry darkness to wintry darkness through a fire-warmed hall. They would follow the new faith because it told them what was before and after the brief life of man.*

---

* In addition, the old gods had charged up against them a long arrears of unanswered prayer and unrequited worship. "None of your people, Eaduine, have worshiped the gods more busily than I," said Corfi the priest, "yet there are many more favored and more fortunate. Were these gods good for anything they would help their worshipers." Whereupon he hurled his spear into the sacred temple of Father Woden and became a Christian. (*History of the English People*, Green—Harper & Brothers, 1881, Vol. I, page 46.)

Peter the Hermit and Bernard inaugurated crusade preaching, which has persisted and emblazoned, since "Dieu Veult," many devices upon its banners. Its power to invest a cherished enterprise with the authority of the divine will has had a perpetual allure for the ardent. The Protestant Reformation inherited and continued all these forms of preaching and rebaptized them into the passions of an embattled church, recast them to suit its needs, and gave them an epoch-making content. For the spoken word of appeal, attack, defense, and explanation is the first weapon and support of any cause which has nothing to build with or fight with save its truth, its passion, and its pregnant power. It is likely to be also the last resource of any dying cause.

I have retold this familiar story for one purpose: To show how preaching has changed and must change with changing times, how the forms of it have been created by the need of Christianity and the church, how the regions which it occupies and the ruling ideas it proclaims are determined for it by all the elements which combine to give character to any historic epoch. It is at any given time, if it be alive at all, the creation of all the forces which combine to make the mind of that period. Directly it has become detached from the contemporaneous need of the church, the tested truth and knowledge of its period, or the vital problems of those to whom it is addressed, it becomes, though it speak with the tongues of men and angels, "sounding brass and clanging cymbals."

III.

Preaching today is neither sounding brass nor clanging cymbals—though these notes are occasionally heard—but it is highly experimental.* An authoritative unity of Christian faith and doctrine controlled preaching from St. Paul on Mars Hill to

---

* It is more than that; it is too largely opportunist.

Canon Liddon on Ludgate Hill. There was wide marginal variation but an unbroken continuity of message. No cleavage went to the bottom—even the cleavage between Roman Catholicism and Protestantism. Bossuet and John Wesley preach essentially the same gospel though their validation of it is different —and not so different after all.

These last three or four paragraphs need qualification. For a long period the changing phases of preaching were determined more by the changing needs and situations of the church than by changes in the ruling ideas of the Western world. The church furnished what ruling ideas there were itself and opposed with an often terrible tenacity any invasion which threatened its monopoly of every field of human interest and thought. Actually it is within the last one hundred years that all this has been changed and Christian preaching has had to reckon with ruling ideas which are not the contribution of the church but the creation of the emancipated and inquiring human mind. Now preaching is being carried, along with religion itself, into regions which, if they be no more than the immemorial regions of human need and human condition, do demand changed approaches, words, understandings, and, more than anything else, extension of the force and vision of Christianity into regions which desperately need an entire Christian sovereignty and as desperately resist it.

It is easier to say all this than to make it precise but we cannot go on without trying. I would say here, and as strongly as I know how, that preaching is the most telling agent in sight by which the most vital need of our time can be met. It is not the only agent but it is the elect agent. In all that concerns the ethical life of the individual or society and has to do with the meanings of life and its nobler motivations, in the final reconciliation of the burden of our souls with the mystery of the universe, our genesis therein and our destiny beyond it, religion holds a place which has heretofore been filled by nothing else. And, if anything else should fill it, that would itself eventually become religion. Preaching has all the more purely intellectual side of all this to itself, though not of course alone. All thought and speech and writing about life in any aspect of it must, if carried far enough and high enough, take on some quality of preaching and come trailing some clouds of religion.

Here are the opportunity and burden of modern preaching. There have been few periods, it seems, more charged with destiny or more discordant than our own. We may be exaggerating our distresses because we are alive to feel them, because we hear so much about them and because all the distresses of all the world say good-morning to us in the newspapers and say good-night to us over the radio. In the remote past civilizations suffered silently, died mutely. There is left no clear record of their agony as their doom fell upon them; nor have we much record of the general mind in such trying periods of change as have heretofore ushered in a new epoch for civilizations which have survived.

It may be we are soft, unduly self-conscious, overly self-pitying. The sharp thrust of the edges of a fractured economic system is probably more keenly felt than in other periods of economic debacle partly because city dwellers and factory workers are now more dependent than ever before on what economists call "long circuit" economics. The farmhouse in which I spent my boyhood could stand a deal of economic strain for it was largely self-contained. One of my early boyhood memories is going with my grandfather to the mill. We took with us wheat of our own harvesting to be ground by the power of a little river from which our valley was named. I remember how the old mill trembled as the stones turned, how the swift water gleamed as I watched it through the cracks of the floor, and how the unbolted flour slowly filled our sack.

I did not know then as I know now how the labor of pioneer ancestors who had won their wheat fields from the forest and asked no more than bread for wages made that grist sacred; how earth and sky were being ground between those stones; how their turning was praise to God; how an epic of humanity ended in that mill. I only knew that they baked our bread when we got home in our own oven and how sweet it was and how there could be no hunger as long as water flowed and wheat ripened. All that and the self-contained village and countryside life—as if there were no world beyond our low and lovely hills—is gone. The river still runs but turns no mills, the fields are still fertile but those who till them take little joy from their harvests. There might be bread enough and to spare—and little children go hungry. The world is interlocked and vulnerable with a perverted power to wound itself.

It is out of this and kindred conditions that our confusion comes. The sensitive Christian mind shares it acutely—far more acutely, I take it, than the patterned economic or financial mind. The reason is clear enough. The patterned economic and financial minds, being the minds of those who have so conspicuously profited by the inherited order, are struggling to maintain it, partly because they have no vision to conceive another and partly because their prestige and unsocial power would go with it. The church is also caught on its institutional side in the same situation and has, besides, its own treasured inheritances of faith or authority which are threatened. But there are sensitive Christian minds and consciences which, though they have given too many hostages to an unchristian order, have no purpose to continue it at the cost of their dearest loyalties, or the surrender of their noblest hopes.

They are acutely conscious also of the dissolving action of pretty much every phase of modern scholarship upon the inherited bases of faith. They face thus an enormous task. They must lay new foundations without, if they can help it, bringing down the structure which shelters them. It is a task far beyond the power of a single generation to achieve.

IV.

Preachers of exceptional genius, like Beecher or Brooks, may come into some new province of preaching with a free, immediate power but the great changes come slowly. They issue confusedly out of situations which involve epochal readjustments. The final outcome is never clearly seen. The actors in the drama do not know the dénouement of their action; their own parts, though set for them by a Power beyond themselves, become evident only as they go on. It is as if Hamlet began to play Hamlet in an unwritten drama which would take form only as he went on, compelled by something more strong than himself and in bonds to himself at the same time. Which is exactly what happens to any Hamlet before a Shakespeare makes a play of him. Then the rightness of the play is due to the playwright's genius to conceive the drama which Hamlet makes of his own life.

Hamlet is not a happy illustration since it was his tragedy to be inadequate to the situations he had to resolve. (Tragedy and comedy are no more than alternative ways of being inadequate.) What is meant is: One does not find one's lines written and ready to be said either in the great dramas of life or history. They have to be discovered. Those who sense most clearly the message of the unseen Dramatist, and anticipate the true action before it is evident, take their part proudly (though not always safely) and creatively. Thereafter it all seems to be what they have said and done.

Preaching is now in much that situation. A vast deal depends upon its prescience and its courage and, above all, on its conception of the ruling ideas by which it charts itself and in which it finds its message. It may wisely therefore engage itself in an examination of these ruling ideas which should now control preaching and make it rightly creative. For preaching must be creative, nobly creative, and, since it is Christian preaching, it must help to create Christian ways of life.

There is always a front in which the Christian and non-Christian, the religious and the non-religious meet and engage. Behind this front are the ultimate heights of the great mysteries and sovereign confidences. The exploration of these regions does not, first of all, belong to the preacher. It belongs to lonely groups who work half lost among the clouds, the bearing of whose labor upon those who use the crowded ways of life seems remote enough. Their conclusions reach and shape us only through the sequent years. The preacher must know what is being done there, being of necessity himself half a citizen of these regions. But his real engagement is with the immediate need of his time.

Is there something, then, which the Christian ministry has now definitely, authoritatively, and creatively to say? It must be something which can withstand the confusions and criticisms of modernity. It should be something whose solidity and power are every day made more manifest through their contrast with the misdirected passion of a weltering world. It must be ample enough to supply preaching a great subject matter, vital enough to touch it with living power, entirely Christian, native to what is most central and timeless in Christianity itself and august with its own innate authority—and it should meet the mood and mind of the time at the central point of their own inadequacy.

If one should call it a Christian philosophy of life it would seem an anticlimax. "Is this," the ardent would answer, "all that preaching has to offer our burning hopes and fears?"

It seems to ask the substitution of speculation for certainty, quest for authority, human wisdom for divine revelation, gnosis for the cross—in short, that is exactly what St. Paul protested against so fervently. "Philosophy" is a word to put any fire out. It suggests detachment just at a time when nearly everybody is so adhesively attached to some project or other as to be unable to see it steadily and see it whole—and unwilling to try.

Philosophy, the generality maintain, is either an escape from reality or an attempt to create an order of reality which has little bearing upon the real business of life. Philosophy is moreover strongly held to be quite the opposite of religion, having no other relation to it than to make its saving passion a pallid ghost. All this is true enough; it is not the whole truth. Philosophy is handicapped by its name. There are given names which it requires the full force of a vigorous personality to live down; titles (like "professor") which practically amount to an indictment in the courts of public opinion. Philosophy is one of those unfortunates—and undeservedly, since to begin with it was almost a street-corner word, being nothing more than a love of wisdom.

It was not cradled on lonely heights. It walked the streets of Athens, clothed in a homespun garment which would probably have been the better for washing, in the person of Socrates who had an incurable passion for wisdom-about-life, ideas of his own about it, and such a gift for kindling a fire for the quest of it in the minds and spirits of Athenian youth that the ardor of the quest has never since been lost. Plato, who continued Socrates' task, never consciously wrote philosophy. He only sought to make men wise about life though he knew when he set out to do it, and knew better as he went on, that his quest would carry him far above the streets of Athens. Wisdom, he knew, has its true dwelling place in high regions and beyond the gates of ivory and horn.

He could not build a "New Republic" beneath the shadow of the Acropolis without seeking a foundation therefor in the unseen and enduring. But he began in Athens. Dante could not appraise the stormy politics of Florence without making his narrow streets coterminous with heaven and hell and carrying the issues of medieval Italy beyond time itself. But he began with Florence. No more can we save our republic save as we carry its affairs beyond our politics and controversies of immediate expediency into regions high above their heat and dust—but we must begin with the heat and the dust. No more can any man now be wise about life who is not wise beyond the narrow foregrounds of his station, his possession, or his task. But he must take his departure from his station and his task and carry them into relationships above and beyond their fugitive estate.

It is this power and necessity to lift the issues of life to their noblest levels which give to philosophy her true empire. If she forgets or deserts her station close to all human ways for cloudy regions of unverifiable speculation and becomes a mere affair of words or a game between men with a genius for supporting their structure with "sky-hooks," so much the worse for them and philosophy. If life finds no interpretation for its experience and no guidance of regnant wisdom, so much the worse for life.*

Every one of us has some wisdom-about-life in obedience to which he lives and acts. It may be fragmentary, out of scale, clear in regions, clouded in regions. It may be so essentially wrong as to involve us and our enterprises in disaster. But in some form or other it is there. It is the result of inheritance, training, experience, and reflection. It is crossed and recrossed by formative influences beyond any man's power to untangle and trace to their sources. Plain men and women who live and

---

* The test of any philosophy, John Dewey has said, is just this: If one can come back from its conclusions to life and find life by their help more luminous and livable, it is right. If its conclusions add confusion to life they are wrong.

work with elemental things and in partnership with the ways
of nature, farmers and seafarers and craftsmen, have often a
grave and weighty wisdom-about-life, shaped through much
slow brooding and tempered in patient bearing of our common
human lot.   Such as these often put the professedly wise to
shame by their insights and understandings.   They too know,
as Plato knew, what far frontiers there are to life and how their
land or sea has unseen horizons.   They are the inheritors of
life's most ancient and elemental wisdom, and through them
and their steadfastness our human enterprise is strong.

V.

When, through some dislocation of the order in which they
live and work, what they trust fails them and what they do
does not support them and they see no sure issue of their toil;
when, concretely, their wisdom-about-life is not adequate to
the enterprises of life, they grow hopelessly confused.   The
essential structure of society begins ominously to be shaken,
and unless the structure is soon and adequately strengthened
in ways which reach the very heart of the strain, blind Samp-
son pulls down the pillars and it falls in some ruinous revolution.   Then a hundred explanations are offered but not often
the ultimate explanation: that a philosophy of life has broken
down.

Whatever is evident about us, whatever is in action among
us is in some form the creation of our wisdom-about-life, or
else our folly-about-life.   Cloud-capped towers and gorgeous
palaces, new Empire State buildings and old Versailles, the desperately poor who built the palace, the packed tenements across
which the shadow of the skyscraper falls, are all aspects incarnate and dominant of the wisdom-about-life of an epoch or
an empire.   They have no other foundation.   So are factories
and navies, constitutions and administrations, the farmer be-

tween his plow handles, the chemist in his laboratory, the saint at prayer, and the preacher in the pulpit.

There are departmental wisdoms, of course: economic—at least there could be; financial—not always in evidence; scientific; technical; what you please. There is often a great soundness in some of the departments, disastrous folly in others. A civilization may be wise in production and unbelievably stupid in distribution. The wisdom of science may be used in the insanity of war. The craftsman makes a bomb or a tool. The protagonists of this or that department may urge its unescapable sovereignty. The economist may hold that economics make history, states, and souls. The scientist may offer his laboratory as the throne-room for humanity, and the technocrat promise the millennium to a world which will let him manage its affairs. They are all right in a way and all wrong in so far as any one of them claims a monopoly of wisdom and administration. They are like the forgotten gods who were once believed to administer little specialized affairs: "departmental gods," half gods, sure to go when the whole gods come.

For we need a master wisdom-about-life always and everywhere: something to do more than coordinate our departmental wisdoms, something to fuse them into a creative unity. They are all subject to something vaster than themselves. They are all within our power to take and use for something beyond themselves; or else they become robots without a humanizing mind, Frankensteins without a humanizing heart. What does it profit to invent and build and organize and drive if we have no envisioned goal? Unless there be a master value to assign all lesser values their station, how can they be stabilized or brought in any kind of order, and unless there is a wisdom-about-life wide-walled enough to include the whole of it, practical enough to press with control upon any situation, with a power to renew and direct our way—

"A star
   To which as to a fountain,
      Other stars returning
   In their golden urns draw light,"

our human endeavors would seem foredoomed to endless confusion and final defeat. Christianity was meant, if one reads
the mind of Jesus aright, to be just that.

Actually Christianity has always had a philosophy at the
heart of it. It has an ethic for conduct, and ethics are always
whatever funded wisdom-about-life we possess. It has an awesome range of creed and doctrine which have always demanded
a philosophic support. All old doctrines were to begin with
some philosophy, some wisdom-about-life invested with a divine
authority, supported by faith and wonder, defended by philosophers who called themselves theologians and who, in time, forgetting how their creeds grew and from what roots, substituted
assertion for insight and repetition for growth. Religion itself
was always wisdom-about-life to begin with. It was, says
Frazier, what passed for wisdom when the world was young.
Its real power has always depended upon the tested insight of
the wisdom at the heart of it. It has had always, if it were to
live at all, to accommodate itself to changes and increases of
wisdom.

The development of religion has always been just this: the
absorption of whatever new wisdom-about-life we have gained
in any region and an enrichment and revitalization of itself
thereby. It cannot escape the challenge of any new thing. It
cannot live if it deny any true thing. Those who believe in
religion believe it has a power to gather back into itself every
tested result of observation, experience, and experiment. It
may as a consequence change or discard once significant aspects
of its reality but it will in the essence of it be thereby purged

and enlarged, and, in return, it will give to what it has taken to itself its ultimate meaning. Without it knowledge and experience are fragmentary and incomplete.

VI.

Now all this bears directly upon preaching. Wisdom-about-life is—or should be—its peculiar province. I mean an inclusive, reconciling, and making-whole * Christian wisdom-about-life. In the region of the interpretation of life and experience, of moral evaluation and leadership, in whatever deals with yesterday's sorrow or tomorrow's surer hope, preaching (I repeat) has a place nothing else can fill. The preacher touches—or should touch—all the edges of life, pressing in on every aspect of life more closely and constantly than anyone else. The physician perhaps gets nearer the raw edges of life than the minister † but the minister shares with the doctor a ministry of healing in all those regions where the soul and mind are also sick, and he has, in addition, a field all his own.

The teacher touches life very closely. So do the social worker and all those whose concern is with the broken human waste of whatever is unhuman in our social order. But the preacher still has a field of his own. Literature may be very wise but relatively few people read for wisdom. Journalism is too largely the servant of causes and interests, artful in prejudices and spurious passion, camouflaged sophistry at its worst, and dealing with society in the mass at its best. Its power is beyond debate, and great journalists have always held their power in trust. But a study of any news-stand will show it all too barren in creative wisdom-about-life and often far too resourceful in sheer foolishness-about-life.

Preaching has always had—has still—and quite literally the

---

* I would say "integrating" but that word is overworked.
† A wise doctor once said to me: "We see people in their night clothes."

"benefit of clergy"; its tonsure is never quite concealed. Whether this is good for preaching or very bad for it I do not know, though it would not be "preaching" without it. A critic might maintain pretty successfully that it was very bad for good preaching since a "sermon" is by some turn of the ungodly mind lightly esteemed in many quarters. "Of course," they say, "a preacher would say that!"—*that* being quite often the most true and pertinent thing which is being said anywhere.

Very often what is clearly and strongly said in the pulpit with an outstanding personality behind it, and reported sketchily in Monday's paper, carries little weight, while what is said in the same issue by an anonymous editor makes public opinion. On the other hand, a very great deal which in the end comes to nothing is heard reverently because the "preacher" says it. As Stephen Blackpool said, "It's a' a muddle."

This at least is clear; preaching is still invested with the awesome authority of religion and the church. It is associated with the great adventure of the soul in prayer. It is prefaced by confession and done in an atmosphere warmed by praise to God. What the preacher says thus carries beyond itself, gaining from the very setting of it and what, in the mind of the congregation, lies behind it, a force which, if it be right, makes it a tremendous instrument and, if it be wrong, saves it from the immediate consequences of its own weakness. The heedless world or the attentive congregation still accepts a sermon as some accent of the Holy Ghost.

If then some sovereign wisdom-about-life is always and everywhere one of our two or three greatest human needs; if one may go so far as to call it a philosophy of life; if religion on both its ethical and doctrinal sides always has been and always must be sovereign wisdom-about-life; if preaching is the voice of it with unique authority and a crucial region all its own; then preaching in a time when it is beginning to slip might save itself (which is not so important) and help save its world (which is terribly important) by helping us all to a wisdom-about-life adequate to the need of the time and worthy of Christian faith and truth.

VII.

If one should trace the portentous aspects of modern society to their true causes he would find them the projection of an inadequate wisdom-about-life against the vast screen of contemporaneous action. Our current wisdom-about-life has somehow and somewhere broken down and threatens to carry with it the vast superstructure of our present social life. It has become menacingly inadequate. Actually the general American philosophy of life is a fusion of inherited Christianity and the gospel of economic getting and "getting on." It would require an analysis for which there is no room here to lay out strand by strand all the threads in our interwoven fabric.

Christianity has answered the three great questions: Whence and Whither and Why. It has furnished an individual ethic of a godly, righteous, and sober life. It has produced generations of good men and women, charitable, devout, good home-makers, and good neighbors. It has comforted the sorrowing and inspired the downcast. It has helped the hard-beset to reconcile the experiences of life with their faith in an all-powerful and good God and thus, having delivered their souls, to go on bravely and hopefully, as they could not otherwise have done. It has held steadily before us the vision of a kinder, juster human order, an ideal always unrealized and always unescapable. It has helped the dying to see, through the shadows gathering deeply about them, a light from beyond the hills of time. It has made final earthly farewells tender with the hope of immortal reunions.

If this wisdom-about-life had been quite detached from social situations and been left to reckon with nothing but what is recasting religion itself and doctrinal Christianity, it would have its own difficulties but, since it is rooted deep in life and life's encompassing mysteries, it would hold its own because there is nothing to take its place. But it has been tied in one bundle with the American gospel of getting on, which is the other element in our current wisdom-about-life.

It has taught an ethic of labor and thrift. Its recompenses has been both heavenly and exceedingly earthly—with possibly not enough between. Success was the principal terrestrial reward of the good life, a very pleasant kind of success; a good house on a good street; an assured future; good children in good schools; a club or so; a gothic church with a preacher to be proud of and good "voices" in the choir; a bank deposit against which to draw benevolent checks, and the happy sense of having won and deserved all of it, as though God recognized a good man when He saw him and did His part.

America has been kind to a religion like that. It worked. We are beginning now to see with a certain critical detachment why it worked and what factors, from a continent waiting to be occupied, developed, and exploited, to an unparalleled upthrust of technical and scientific knowledge, made it possible. The historian of the future may possibly tell what halted and undid it and what happened thereafter.

This inherited and hitherto partially adequate wisdom-about-life has issued in pathetic confusion. As far as it was and is a system of Christian doctrine, it has grown remote to the believing, difficult enough to the questing, incredible to the critical. As far as it was and is an individual ethic, it finds itself entangled in a social ethic of an alien character. As far as it was a happy and successful way of life, it is being undone by forces beyond its control, and there is an uneasy sense among us that the defeat is far more than an episode in the economic cycle.

I would not make the picture too dark. I would only stress the urgency of the situation and the challenge and opportunity it offers preaching. There is a brief pathetic passage in the Fourth Gospel. The world was turning away from Jesus. He stood lonely and sad before receding tides which, it seemed, not even His boundless affection could halt and turn. "Will ye also go away?" He said to the handful who were left, and Peter answered, "Lord, to whom shall we go?"

There are always times when the receding tide must ask that question and find an answer. The current of human aspiration and endeavor can never be content to do no more than empty in some "unplumbed, salt, estranging sea" of disillusionment and aimless confusion. It wants an object, a control, some glowing sense of meaning in its movement. Unless all our faith is a dream and the demonstration of the centuries of no account, Christianity has in the Way, the Truth, and the Life of Jesus Christ a wisdom-about-life for which there was never greater need.

Preaching is the interpretative voice of just that. If it can meet the occasion its mission was never more clearly defined. If not, the church and the pulpit in it will hear through its doors receding voices saying, "Where *shall* we go?" The pulpit has an answer: "Let us seek together a Christian wisdom-about-life to find out where we are meant to go and what we may become as we go. Let us undertake together the quest for Christian-mindedness. Have that mind in you which was also in Jesus Christ."

CHAPTER IV

EMPTY THRONE-ROOMS

IF ONE maintains that the most important business of Christian preaching at present is to make Christian-minded individuals and a Christian-minded society, he would better take care about his definition of mind. It must include the emotional as well as the purely intellectual—if there is any such thing—the "heart" as well as the "head" since the "heart" may be a more strategic region than the "head" and far more difficult to capture. A man will change his ideas sooner than his prejudices, and surrender everything in a conviction save the emotions which keep it alive. At the same time preaching would just now better drive for the intellect rather than the emotions, the mind rather than the mood.

The tendency of evangelical religion is to drive for the emotions first, the will next, and let the intellect make what terms for itself which it can when they are taken. Most religious apologetic is just now backing the "heart" against the "head." It is risky business. The only sure correction for wrong moods is a right mind. A hard intellectualism needs an emotional flux but directly an age begins to rationalize its emotions the sky is the limit. The result is the dangerous emotional instability now so much in evidence. The task of the church is to establish among us the sovereignty of Christian-mindedness.

One must confess directly that this seems far too simple a prescription for our sicknesses. The Socratic fallacy, we used to be told, was assuming that because a man knew the good he would do it. Socrates himself would have recognized the gap which often opens tragically between wisdom and wise action or between the knowledge of the good and goodness. He would likely have argued, however, that one should keep on trying to help men toward wisdom and right knowledge of the good since without them there would be, so to speak, no abutments to work from in trying to bridge the gap. And he would, one imagines, being wise himself, have included in his "good" the impulse as well as the understanding and the will as well as the mind. They are all actually a seamless robe.

The "heart" of the Old and New Testaments is the whole man in source and action, "thoughts, passions, desires, appetites, affections, purposes, endeavors." The agent of their conjoint action is the will, the result is what we are. The modern psychologist would probably be willing to make "mind" inclusive enough for such a definition of the "heart." Christianity makes its appeal to all these aspects of our strangely tangled natures and asserts its empire over them all. There is ample room here for every line preaching can take. "Evangelical" preaching is the "heart" of the Christian gospel but even it must begin or end with a Christian wisdom adequate to the conduct of Christian life in a world like ours. Christian-mindedness needs greatly to be enlarged but the creation of it might be just now the supreme and strategic task of Christian preaching.

St. Paul who, above all men, needed a sovereign strategy, being on fire to capture for his Master just the one thing in human nature which carried the whole man with it, came back more than once to Christ-mindedness as the crucial Christian attitude. There were, he recognized, and sadly, other minds, fleshly and worldly, vain, stained, and divisive, which it was a Christian's business to get rid of. The only way to get rid of them was to put another mind in their place, establish the mind of Christ in the throne-room of personality. St. Paul had a sound psychology though he did not know the word; he simply knew human nature. He knew that it could not be dealt with negatively or kept piously empty; that the only way to get rid of wrong-mindedness with its complex of emotions and motivations was to supplant it with a positive right-mindedness.

He invested that transaction with a mystic splendor, he approached it from all the ranges of his faith and the mystery of the cross. But when he came down from the heights he spoke quite simply: "What I mean and insist upon in the Lord's name is this; you must no longer live like the heathen, with their frivolity of mind and darkened understanding. You must lay aside your . . . old self. . . . You must adopt a new attitude of mind. Have this mind in you which was also in Jesus Christ." And he went into plain detail about the content of that new mind. There was the source of the power which was to change the world. It was Paul's task to begin it.

It is now the preacher's task to continue it. He cannot do it with a phrase, and he cannot do it at all unless he has himself some controlling conception of what the Christian mind ought to be here and now. What are the ruling ideas of it? And the ruling motivations? And its distinguishing spirit? How does it bear upon contemporaneous situations? How can it build roads for itself from its essentially Christian idealism to some realization of them in an order it has hardly yet begun to make essentially Christian? What answer has it for all the shadowed side of life? How can it relate itself to the mind of science? And other phases of the modern mind? These are burning questions. They involve, from the Christian approach, every aspect of our individual and social life.

The answer if pressed home drives straight at the heart of almost contemporaneous situations. A preacher cannot deliver a sermon which does not touch some aspect of them. No preacher is equal to all of these things and his best will be humbled by unescapable fallibilities. But he is one of a very great company, and if there should be among the entire Christian ministry a cooperative effort to create among us a Christian-mindedness, a Christian wisdom-about-life fitted to the needs of which we are all conscious, something of tremendous import would get done.

I.

Preaching might, therefore, advantageously substitute a Christian wisdom-about-life for inherited doctrinal preaching. It might turn out to be doctrinal preaching in the end but it would have an appeal which purely doctrinal preaching does not now possess. It would furnish preaching the articulated and supporting thought-structure which systematic theology supplied earlier generations and without which sermons tend to become a disconnected series of observations, exhortations, "efforts" preached out of necessity, expediency, the concordance, last week's newspaper, the last book read, or the last monthly issue of First Aid to Preaching.

Systematic theology did supply, and for the doctrinal-minded today does supply, the structural framework of ruling ideas which make preaching vertebrate. Something must save preaching from a pulpy kinship to the jellyfish. The figure is worth pressing. Some sermons float bravely in summer seas—though too much like the medium in which they float—but once they meet the coasts of life, and the tides which bore them in have turned home again, there is left of them only a jelly on the sand. You would not think so beautiful a thing could become nothing so soon.

All this tenacious interwoven play of experience (so many kinds of experience) and encompassing reality (so many kinds of reality) which we call life cannot be met and mastered and organized into wisdom and power by anything less than a system of understanding, within whose frame all the forces of life can be victoriously resolved. The deeply thoughtful have always known this. The supremely gifted have sought to give to some sufficiently inclusive philosophy of life a permanent form, and left their systems like a mountain range against the horizons of the human mind. From them streams of character and consequence have flowed down through the centuries.

There are five great philosophies of life, William DeWitt Hyde said once in a book of rare insight: * The Epicurean Pursuit of Pleasure, Stoic Self-Control by Law, Platonic Subordination, The Aristotolean Sense of Proportion, and The Christian Spirit of Love. No one of these philosophies is actually the unaided creation of a master mind. It is the final formulation around some one ruling idea of the habits, attitudes, quests, and confidences which are interwoven through the whole of human life and action. The philosophy does no more than give them unity and justify command.

If Dr. Hyde had traced the course of these philosophies through history and religion and ethics—an impossible task— with the effect of them upon character and institutions, he would have accounted for dominant aspects of great civilizations and proved that the rise or dissolution of such philosophies marks epochs in human enterprises. He would have taught us that a society without an adequate wisdom-about-life becomes anarchical. That philosophies of life right and wise in some phases of them and wrong or unbalanced in other phases create unbalanced states and souls. That whoever envisages, shapes, and releases a wisdom-about-life with a power to displace the old and increasingly assert its empire becomes the lord of uncalendared years.

* *The Five Great Philosophies of Life*—William DeWitt Hyde, The Macmillan Company, New York, 1911. By permission of The Macmillan Company.

Jesus, Dr. Hyde maintained, did just that. But he took great care to say and say clearly that the "faith of the world has found in Jesus much more than a philosophy of life." * The church bells which are filling the bright Thanksgiving morning on which this is being written with their antiphonals are a testimony to that. It would be as unfair and untrue to reduce Christianity to a life philosophy as to reduce their music to mere vibrations of bell-metal. The slow beating of their sonorous notes measures out memory and hope. They pulse with mystic association. They are the voices of two thousand years of faith, devotion, quest, and peace. The crosses beneath which they ring are symbols of what lies beyond the power of any philosophy to define.

II.

And yet—— Christianity must actually lay hold of life through the essential rightness and finality of its wisdom-about-life. If its ruling ideas are inapplicable to the whole of life in its long sequences; if it is really built upon foundations which experience and tested knowledge can dissolve; if the conduct of life and the stability of society cannot be fitted enduringly into the frame of it; if its claim to supremacy will finally be defeated by a philosophy of life more entirely suited to emergent conditions, then, though the church bells keep ringing, they will be less and less heard and obeyed. Those who anticipate their eventual silence must not leave out of account the tenacities of religion and the persistence of its summons. The temple bells of Mandalay, the call to prayer from minarets, the music from Christian spires and towers have outlasted dynasties, empires, and cultures. They will keep sounding on and

---

* "Yet Jesus' Spirit of Love is the final philosophy of life. . . . Of course such a limitation to his philosophy of life leaves out of account all supernatural and eschatological considerations. We here consider only the truth and worth of the teaching. . . ." *Ibid.*—Preface.

on. The pity would be not that they should be silenced but that their voices should become remote with no actual command over the tides of life beneath—*vox et præterea nihil*—a voice and nothing more.

And that is happening. To say why is to re-examine religion—any religion—in its relation to the entire content of the culture to which it belongs. I do not think it an extreme generalization to say that one would always discover at the core of any religion, threatened with the possibility of dissolution, either a philosophy of life which will not stand against experience or stand up under examination, or else that its followers have not lived it out and up and on. And always one will discover, in the shadows which begin to gather about it, the emerging form of another and competitive philosophy of life.

Western civilization and all the regions reached and influenced by Western civilization are caught and shaken and near undone by an engagement of philosophies of life which in some phases have become a battle to the death. The debacle of civilization beginning a decade before the World War has been at the tragic heart of it just a conflict in the regions of the imponderable, projected against all the horizons of world history in unresolved strife and revolution.

Every outstanding contemporaneous social or economic experiment either justifies itself by a philosophy already in action or is creating a philosophy to commend it. The confusion and exaggeration of these philosophies must not blind us to their significance. Neither Mussolini nor Hitler can recast ancient states without a philosophy to build on or else an idealism to hallow the structure. Italian Fascism has now secured a definite philosophy.* Hitler seems to have left out the philosophic

---

* See, for example, *Making the Fascist State*—Herbert W. Schneider, Oxford University Press, New York, 1928, pp. 238-253 and appendix part I.

stage and driven straight and hard for the holy achievement of a Teutonic religion with a Germanic god and Hitler as his prophet. In fact, among the more pious Hitlerite theologians the Chancellor has become a savior. "Christ has come to us through Adolph Hitler. . . . Every happening is of two fold nature: internal and external. Today we feel it; the savior has come to us." Old evangelical Germany finds it difficult at this writing to accept all the implications of this particular incarnation, and the state is beginning to be shaken.

Here we have the whole sequence in plain historic sight: a revolution which cannot do without a philosophy, and the philosophy itself becoming a religion—the religion of "race" and "blood." The new movements cannot dethrone the inherited order unless the sheer pride and will-to-power in them be hidden by a religious garmenture. The increasing use of the word "mystic" in both Italian and German state philosophy is as evident as it is significant. It is an attempt to secure for the new religion of nationalism the sanction of a very old personal piety and to glorify a realistic politic with a supernal light. Also, as in many more orthodox uses of the word, it enables the user to escape the inconvenience of honest thought and definite statement.

III.

One does not need to go to Europe for illustration. Our contemporaneous American life is seamed by embattled philosophies. They are not thus named in so many plain words. They are a conflict of systems, parties, sections, and interests. They are in the NRA and in its critics; they are in the long front between the employing and employed groups where a truce is no sooner secured in one sector than fighting breaks out in another. They are in the bitter fight taking changing forms between debtor and creditor groups. They are in the lynching mobs which bestialize themselves in the torture of the bestial.* They are in the profound tension between the militarist and the pacifist, between contestant conceptions of government; their unseen frontiers run through the church itself.

They are incarnate in the minds of the younger generation of preachers. Their doctrinal uneasiness has many contributing elements, some of which cannot be ignored save at the price of their intellectual integrity. They are caught between a past Christianity which inheritance and training have wrought into the very fiber of them and a future Christianity whose outlines are still too dim and distant to call them clearly from its radiant heights. They are seeking to reconcile new social and economic and ethical philosophies with inherited reverences and loyalties. Their preaching and their writing reveal their confusion. They are idealists skeptical of the actual power of an ideal. They are realists who make a romance of realism. Some of them have a definite program. Others have found as yet no resolution of their divided selves and making a gospel of "tension" preach it brilliantly, though what they say is more significant as a disclosure of inner schism than creatively helpful.

A later time, with the advantage of seeing both the event and the issue, will trace much of this back to its source in the want among us of a philosophy of life inclusive enough to contain all the elements which must in some way be disposed of, with the power to make a whole out of our fragmentary experiences and efforts, commanding enough to take creative control of all our affairs and so deeply right as to bring with it an enduring and blessed rightness.

Christian faith believes that the Christian wisdom-about-life, and that alone, can meet the world's need. It is articulate in the teachings of Jesus. It is rich in the contributions of the

---

* This I think is a slander on the animal world. There is a factor of cruelty in human nature which cannot be matched in the jungle.

Christian mind and the demonstration of a long and noble experience. It would be as impossible to disassociate it clearly from
theologies and sacraments, the hymn books and the prayer
books, the authority of the church and the testimony of the
saved, as to return again to earth and air in due proportion all
the elements which have been built into a tree. But beneath
and through all this there is a philosophy of life whose ruling
ideas can be discovered and set in order. They can be and
must be addressed to the mind, to begin with, though in their
issue they must command the will and furnish a channel for
the emotions.

Their demonstration, since they are a philosophy of life, is
in life itself. The field of their application is the whole of our
endeavor, and the test of their truth is and will be their power
to take and transform our troubled selves and our troubled ways.
There is not a lonely sorrow for which they do not have a message of comfort, nor a shadow for which they have not a master
light, nor any impasse of the nations out of which they will
not open a road, nor any entanglement in folly or in fault from
which they will not supply deliverance. Their rightness of
truth has been twice proved: once by the solidity of whatever
in the last two thousand years has at all conformed to their command, once by the confusion and defeat which attend the denial
and neglect of them.

They are, I suppose, not so much ruling ideas as ruling attitudes, though they do demand intelligence and often a very
discriminating intelligence in the application of them to situations. Love, said St. Paul, is the greatest of them, no single
or simple thing but the sum in action everywhere of all those
qualities whose recital makes the great passage into which he
breaks the whole light of it a many-banded spectrum. Such
qualities seem too delicate for life's rough needs, but they have
demonstrated their power to meet and break the drive of what,

unchecked, wrecks all the gracious commerce of life. And yet to ask, using a single example, what the glowing good-will St. Paul calls love would do with the gray city of buried alive living men whose walls I have only to turn a corner to see* is to make a demand as yet unmet upon the intelligence of the state.

The Christian philosophy of life is a "heart" philosophy as well as a "head" philosophy, but it is not to be reasoned out of court for all that. I have said already that our dominant need is right-headedness and that right-headedness makes right-heartedness but love has a wisdom all its own and a penetrating discernment. Its methods may sometimes be foolish but they never have the disintegrating stupidity of hate-ways and pride-ways. The shadow of ourselves darkens all our councils. Only as we get clear of those shadows can we discover how to resolve any situation in which competitive interests are involved. The real barriers between us and the Realm of God are not in our institutions but in our souls. They are our fear, our pride, our narrow-visioned selfishness. We project these into all our enterprises and give them force and form through our unwillingness to recognize them for what they are.

IV.

They are obstacles of a very stubborn sort for all that. It is far easier to tunnel a mountain or bridge an estuary of the sea than get an open road through long, tenaciously established, interlocking group attitudes or bring to one mind the representatives of enmities almost as old as history. Human nature is not—

> ". . . an idle ore
> But iron shaped in central gloom
> And heated hot with burning fears
> And dipped in baths of hissing tears
> And battered with the shock of doom."

---

* Auburn State Prison.

For once a poet has spoken with scientific restraint—Tennyson often did. No wonder we are hard to fuse and recast.

We seem so slow to be enkindled by what needs time and patience, so quick to take fire about little things never worth the passion we spend upon them as to make one wonder whether we are capable of the sustained and costly emotions needed for the supreme Christian ideals. How, for example, can we ever secure international peace as long as a fluttering flag above a steel helmet bares our heads and quickens our very pulse beat while a wind-blown flag over a plowshare would leave us cold? A sword-flash is poetry, courage, and song; a plowshare turning April sod is only an earth-stained tool—and yet we live by the plowshare and die by the sword. How strange we are even to ourselves as though we kept our music and salutes for death! *

An artist with Detailles' art and far more than Detailles' vision might paint upon the walls of the choir in the pantheon of humanity a nobler picture than "Vers La Gloire" in the Paris pantheon. For the plowshare has led a procession which puts the retinue of glory and the sword to shame. Its users have worn homely garments and lived near the homely things of earth. They have gone out to meet the sunrise around the world, they have had no company as they came home but weariness and lengthening shadows. But civilization has sprung from its furrows, beauty and contentment have attended its slow procession. High clouds have furnished it a flag, and the sound of wind through the corn has made for it a happy music.

The sword has done no more for it than change the overlords of the lands it plows, ride down their harvests, and water their ruin with blood. Now and then a prophet like Isaiah has anticipated its victory over the sword, a poet like Hardy seen its

---

* That, I suppose, is not quite true. We on the sidewalk salute courage and, possibly, security in the sword.

immemorial power to outlast empires—and even Hardy sings
but sadly—

> "Only a man harrowing clods
> In a slow silent walk
> With an old horse that stumbles and nods
> Half asleep as they stalk."

"Only"—only labor and love and seed and earth and sky! Yet
these are the enduring things;

> "War's annals will fade into night
> Ere their story die."

V.

All this seems a far cry from preaching and its Christian wisdom-about-life. But it does illustrate how much more the
Christian wisdom-about-life is than simply an ethic or a philosophy. It is no simple matter to live wisely. What wisdom we
have seems only a gleam through the shadows. It is, at its
best, only one of the elements which shape our souls and our
societies. And yet, unless we build upon some foundation of
wisdom, we build upon the sand—and we are not so helpless as
we think. There is at our service a vast, tested, dearly bought
wisdom. It is fundamentally the creation of experience. The
laws and necessities of it are deep in the nature of life, in the
order of the world, in the birth and death of stars. It has been
clarified and given form by the reflection of the wise, and lifted
to summits of command by the insight of the inspired.

We have never been left without those who by some grace of
the spirit or gift of God have had a wisdom to furnish a lamp
for our feet and a light on our paths. Those to whom this
gleam has been given have been the heralds of all our dawns,
the master lights of all our seeing. When after unbelievable
toil we have reached some summit their vision foresaw, we find

them waiting for us there with compassion because we have been so slow, rather than an indignation, for which they might well be pardoned, that we have been so stupid. If they pardon us we should not pardon ourselves, for in the light of all the wisdom we have we ought not to be so stupid as we are. Those to whom this gleam has been vouchsafed have always found the ultimate source of it in religious faith. Even if they have begun with nothing more than wisdom enough for the first stage of the enduring quest, they have found themselves before their quest was done—

> ". . . on those high table-lands
> Whereof our God is moon and sun."

Of all these, by the demonstration of the centuries, Jesus Christ was incomparably the greatest. He began with religion where religion at its then best left off. He did not escape or apparently seek to escape aspects of religion which belonged to His race and His time, but He detached from them their timeless values and bequeathed these to His followers and to the future. His wisdom was made luminous in His teaching, it was glorified by His life and given by His death an appeal to win the world. Whether there was, in the Aramaic He spoke, a word like philosophy I do not know, but He had a wisdom-about-life which plumbed the depths and which He never learned from the schools. His brief ministry lay between a craftsman's shop and the cross. His secret, which the creeds of Christendom have sought in vain to define, lay in what St. Paul called the wisdom from above. He broadcast that gleam. The source of it was in Himself. He was not only the Way and the Truth, He was the Life.

Then something happened. The sequences and consequences of history made of the religion which calls Him Lord and Master less a religion of His luminous wisdom-about-life and His

sureness of God than a religion of salvation focused upon His
sacrificial death. His teaching was always there; His clear
vision of the true, right way of life was always there. It was
never so much overlain as not to be the norm, the treasure, and
too often the reproach of the Christian church. But it was subordinate to the drama of redemption, subordinate to wonder
and speculation about His person. It has never been central in
the creeds, it has always been a pendant to massive theologies
drawn in part from sources to which His own mind was alien—
theologies which have been concerned in part with matters about
which He never said a recorded word.

And all the while the sad reproach of His words came back
as echoes from the Palestinian hills, "Why call ye me Lord, Lord,
and do not the things that I say?" Preaching must turn these
echoes into living words again and make them regnant. "Christianity of this simple, vital sort is the world's salvation. Criti-
cized by enemies and caricatured by friends; . . . mingled with
all manner of exploded superstition, false philosophy, science
that is not so, and history that never happened; obscured under
absurd rites; . . . evaporated by mystics; stereotyped by literalists;
. . . it has lived in spite of all the grave clothes its unbelieving
disciples have tried to wrap around it, and holds the keys of
Eternal Life." *

Whatever qualification these probably overwritten and hard-
hitting sentences demand is granted. The ethic of Jesus has
created Christian character abundantly, continuously. It has
had for the most part to do its work in an alien setting, been
checked and deflected. In the time scale of human history the
two thousand unfinished years of the gospel are the narrowest
of margins against incalculable millenniums. The best the
West had when St. Paul took ship for Macedonia was a high
and half-hopeless Stoic courage touched by tremulous lights

* Hyde, *Ibid.*, page 291.

and shadows of Platonic idealism. Beyond Rome and Greece
was a girdle of northern forest populated with skin-clad folk
who had won out in the struggle for existence against the ice-
age and the saber-toothed tiger. It has not been easy to take a
world like that and subject it to the Sermon on the Mount,
or redirect into Christian channels the fierce Western will-to-
power. In spite of all this, Christianity has created a beauty of
Christian character which has been the light of the Western
world, a body of creative good with enough Christian salt in
it to more than save society from going rotten.

Beyond debate also Christian doctrine centering about the
drama of redemption has had a power to advance Christianity
as it never could have been otherwise advanced. The fate of
such early forms of Christianity as found in Jesus only a teacher,
and the status of the Friends fellowship which is now the most
conspicuous endeavor to live in all relationships by the Gospels
are proof enough of that. Proof enough, authoritative voices
would say, to close the question; and yet the more critical are
not so sure. For certain aspects of Christian thelogy and insti-
tutionalism have always outrun the Christian transformation of
character and society.

What Jesus said about the two foundations for a man's house
of life is equally true of His church—"Whosoever heareth these
sayings of mine and doeth them, I will liken him to a wise
man which built his house upon a rock." The church has
always known that passage—and looked to the spread of its walls
and the lift of its fretted towers instead of the solidity of its
foundations. No wonder it fears the rising storm.

VI.

With the noblest obedience possible to Jesus' wisdom-about-
life, the Christian church would still be facing a situation to
challenge all its power and wisdom and its courage as well. The

sheer drive of technical industry and the profound changes in habit and grouping attendant upon it have outrun all our power to control and humanize let alone spiritualize them.   The sociologist now calls such aspects of our portentously uneven advance "lags." They are more than that; they are a strain between economic achievement and mass organization and the true values of life which threatens, if it cannot be corrected, the dissolution of a proud epoch.*

Every contemporaneous force which seeks a human and humane control over the mechanism of life is "lagging." Education is struggling desperately to overtake situations which have got beyond it. Politics lag, statesmen lag, and the statesmen who do have some vision of the exigency of their task are attacked—usually from the rear—by those who are not only determined to pull down the pillars of their particular temples over their own heads, but bitterly resent any interference with their blind tugging and pulling. No wonder the Way, the Truth, and the Life of Jesus lag.

But the deeper forces are with it. It is as if life had two currents, not side by side like the Rhone and the Arve for a little, but the one fretted and windswept and facile on the surface, and the other far below unresting and unhasting. Religion is only one aspect of the culture level to which it belongs. It cannot too far outrun or outclimb the world in which it is entangled though its prophets may herald as yet unrisen dawns. And these are often enough scorned for their vision and stoned for their high hopes. This unescapable entanglement of religion with the general mind and the more definite entanglement of religious institutions with society must always be taken into consideration in any adjudication of what Christianity has done or left undone.

---

* Here in America, the menace of the underworld and a seamy lawlessness reaching from high finance to blind-pigs darken the picture.

The church, like most other human institutions, lives on more than one level. There is an ideal church, in the vivid phrase of St. Paul the "body of Christ;" a church having no mind but His, in the world but not of it, being above its clamor and apart from its passion, with a right through its ideal wisdom and goodness to judge the world. The ideal of a church like this has sustained the faith and courage of all believers, the towers of it rise like a dream and a possibility always unrealized above our shadows into a golden light. This is the church of Christian hymns and prayers. It is also the church which the critical assume when they blame organized Christianity for its faults and failures, and the over-ardent assume when they sing its praises.

It exists actually only as any ideal exists—the ideal America, the ideal school, or any other alluring generalization which we can neither live without nor make concrete. The real church always has been and always will be a fellowship of very human folk with limited vision beyond their own horizons and less power to escape or direct the confluence of forces which beat upon the little coasts of their lives. If their religion gives them hope and courage, opens for them a road through the unknown, and keeps alive within them a divine discontent with whatever is untrue to the vision it offers, it does to that degree what it was meant to do. If they surrender to the drive of alien forces, if they cannot foresee the long issue of what they are doing and choose wrong turnings at the forks of the roads of destiny, it is only because they are human, to be pitied rather than blamed, and taught rather than scourged.

The just occasion for blame comes when the Christian church refuses to profit by experience, or, actually possessing some heavenly vision, refuses to obey it. The church is also at fault when it refuses to recognize what is actual in the mind of its time and make such adjustments of message as its mission demands. Then there is no excuse for it save moral lethargy and intellectual obscurantism—which are no excuses at all but indictments.

It has always paid a bitter price for such mishandling of what is committed to it, though any friend of the church who brings historical perspective to his judgments of it must recognize that it has never had an entirely free hand with the world. It is greatly dependent upon changes in general understanding and outlook for its own moral and spiritual advances. It creates in part the tides by which it is lifted and carried, but never entirely. And too often when its mariners should feel beneath them the surge of some finer, freer force, their reminiscent vision is so fixed upon the harbors from which they set sail that they will not commit themselves to what might bring them to their desired haven—and they lose the tide.

VII.

That might be the exact situation of the Christian church today. There is no mistaking its strategic opportunity, or the difficulties the opportunity brings with it. For perhaps the first time in its history it is now reasonably possible for Christianity to offer its entire wisdom-about-life to an age capable of understanding it and greatly concerned about issues upon which it might be brought to bear. All the contact lines are open.

There has been in the last one hundred years an immeasurable growth in social intelligence. Human folk are ceasing to be altogether unconsidered counters in a blind and cruel game. We are beginning to see them in their capacity for suffering and happiness as living souls with soul value. There is an increasing sensitiveness to human ill-being and well-being. There is everywhere about us the slow emergence of a discriminating intelligence asking guidance. We begin to see a little the consequences of the inhuman ways of war and greed and pride of power. We are beginning slowly but unescapably to think of all our enterprises in moral terms. In spite of individual reaction against pattern morality we are beginning to understand with Bishop Butler that morality is the nature of things. But what morality?

Human life has grown warm at the center, it has grown cold and lonely on all the margins of it which touch its vast, encompassing universe. Beneath the incalculable distances of Betelgeuse or Alcyone it thinks itself alone in the drift of the cosmic tide and forgets how near and glowing love is, or how the great human duties have nothing to do with the fixed stars save to be instructed by their steadfastness and quieted by their imperturbable calm.

The mystery of life and the world which it has always been the province of religion to explore and interpret remains unresolved. Science has only intensified it, brought it closer to the roads we travel and to our own souls. An age sorely confused about religion has a hunger which, though it takes strange and paradoxical forms, is still a questing for God and religion. But what religion?

This is Christianity's opportunity. It has the chance now to be really Christian and richly Christian and transformingly Christian. The time is ripe for it, the level of human understanding and idealism is rising, has risen, to a bench-mark which now for the first time makes possible a consistent release of the whole potential content of Christian idealism. No one can say that it will be easy, or quickly done or ever entirely done. There must always be for both realist and idealist an unrealized margin, or else the realist would have nothing to disown and the idealist nothing to seek.

We shall find little help just now from those who tell us that our efforts are foredoomed to defeat through the unescapable entanglement of moral men in an immoral society. We would better at least try to get more moral men with something besides an inherited pietistic or intransigent morality before we decide what they can or cannot do. No one who goes out to fight for the supreme values can ever hope to occupy the whole field but he can refuse to be turned aside by minor issues. Marlborough and Prince Eugene won Blenheim by sending off Prince Louis comfortably to besiege Ingolstadt according to the rules of the game, while they drove in on the Grand Army of France and kept driving in.

Here then is a world of power and contradiction. It has a conscience about war and plans to fight. It is convicted of economic sin and recoils from bringing forth the fruits of repentance. Its ideals haunt it, its failures sadden it. It wastes precious loyalties and misdirects its own passions. It cannot do without an altar, but sacrifices to strange gods. It is wise enough to weigh the stars and does not know the things which belong to its own peace. It is pathetically eager to be taught and strangely slow to learn from any experience. It calls itself realistic and is lapped by the tides of mystery. The key to it all, beyond what has been so constant in human nature, would seem to be a want of inner unity, the dissolution of our former wisdom-about-life and whatever gave that wisdom commanding appeal and the want, as yet, of a sovereignty of wisdom and purpose adequate to the realms it has to administer. But what sovereignty?

We live in a world of empty throne-rooms in almost every inner and outer region of life. There are few inherited regnancies which are not shaken, few inherited authorities which are not challenged. More than once in the last twenty years we have seen the decorous surface of civilization give way and have looked down into the raw ferocities of a nature we thought had gone with the saber-toothed tiger. Confidences and controls have slipped away from their seats of administration like shadows when the sun is gone. There are empty throne-rooms of the heart with the great loyalties and affections asking for something worth their inestimable value for them to spend themselves upon.

Mussolini is said to have explained in one dramatic sentence his ascent to power: "Europe," he said, "was full of empty thrones. I simply walked in and sat down on one." That sentence short-circuits a revolution but it is true. No judicious writer will let a glowing figure of speech betray him. Nor overstate his case. But there are significant regions of life— the most significant—waiting for the order and peace which can come only from the occupation of the throne-room of the human spirit by a power equal to the need and force of such a world as ours. The Christian church believes the Way, the Truth, and the Life of Jesus Christ equal to the challenge. And it sees nothing else which is equal to the challenge. Can Christianity take the throne-room?

CHAPTER V

THE ROOTS OF PREACHING

PREACHING to the modern mind should, then, fall into two categories: the interpretation—there should be a better word —of life in terms of the Christian revelation; the creation —as far as preaching can create it—of a society conformed to the Christian mind. The difficulty is to do it. Preaching is not only caught in the strain between Christian ideology and the world as a going concern; it is caught in the strain between preaching as it ought ideally to be and the necessity of getting congregations enough to support the preachers themselves, expensively organized churches, and the costly overhead of sectarianism. There is consequently a brisk demand among the generality of preachers for what they can quickly and brightly turn into a sermon.

The faculty to give a new turn to an old text or find a new text for an old turn is highly esteemed. Many clever and some positively brilliant first aids to preaching are available, though their brilliancy is sometimes the dancing light of something bright waved rapidly in the air rather than the steadfast light of a star. A teacher of preaching would be the last person to deny their usefulness. He can only envy the sheer genius of some of his fellow-craftsmen in finding sermons in passages he himself has read and maybe re-read with never that electric shock out of which—as Oliver Wendell Holmes said poetry is born—telling preaching is also born. The men who possess this faculty put their less fortunate brethren in a debt to them which is more often capitalized than acknowledged. Some telling use of an unusual text, like the shot of Concord's embattled farmers, is finally heard around the world. To ask preaching to leave this insistent and really fascinating occupation in which any preacher will confess he finds his "thrills" for an approach which cannot easily be headlined—which as a matter of fact no up-to-date "religious editor" will headline— is asking a good deal.

Lloyd George has just been telling, in his engaging memoirs, how he pleaded with Kitchener to release from front-line service skilled mechanics enough to make the machines to make the munitions without which the front line was only an heroic and tragically futile rendezvous with death. And nobody from Kitchener to the mud-crusted private could see it. How can a soldier on the firing-line leave his weapons and go back to forge even more and more telling ones? What will happen to the line? Actually that is not the preacher's alternative today. His task would be more simple if it were. He has to use his weapons and forge them as he uses them. He must be both Vulcan forging the thunderbolts and Jove discharging them still hot from their creative fires—or something more or less like that.

The action is rarely so spontaneous as the congregation would like to believe but preaching without some such action would cease to be preaching. Beyond debate the temper of the time has heightened the appeal of preaching adapted to a vivid publicity and rewarded the men who possess it with station and renown. No critic of preaching should quarrel too much with that. But the friends of preaching should recognize that it is not enough. There must be a cause somewhere for the gap between the variety and vigor of the American pulpit and the ranges of American life which seem unreached and unchanged by it. Even preachers who take the long view and work for the creation of a society conformed to the Christian mind do not agree in their approach.

Without a regenerated human nature, the evangelical contend, the regenerated state is a dreamer's dream; they want sinners converted. Without a Christian social intelligence and motivation not yet in sight, the less dogmatic maintain, we have no real foundation for a Christian economic structure; they want the ignorant instructed. Our present social order, say the radical, defeats both the converted and instructed; they want society rebuilt. The world is doomed, say the "Barthians," and a Christian can do no more than through his faith seek the Eternal. The result is confusion rather than conviction and more argument at headquarters than action on the line. Preaching, whether it be the Sunday-to-Sunday way of any preacher anywhere or the religious voice of a stormy epoch, needs a general command.

I.

There are definitions of preaching to suit every need, but, whatever it is or is not, it must meet life at some point with some creative message for life. Any preacher's preaching will be, in the continuing substance of it, a revelation of his understanding of life. It will be also the expression of his Christian faith in all its relation to life and its meaning for life, and it must be strongly based. If his preaching is to spread an unfailing and many-branched growth to the sky, it must have an ample rooting. A tree is a useful though hazardous analogy. I do not know what proportion of the maple which furnishes me a lovely calendar of the changing seasons is earth-hid; the entire root-spread of a great tree is rarely uncovered. I only know it maintains a vital balance between its life in the light and its hidden and earth-bound life. If it should get a growth too ample for its root-hold, it is at the mercy of the storm; if its roots maintain no lovely and fruitful growth open to the sky, they will die and rot in the dark.

There are sure to be with any preacher's growth considerable changes in his homiletic root-hold; otherwise he would not grow. What feeds his preaching will change with the changing years. Soils will grow thin and he will strike his roots into another richer soil. Altered conditions will have to be met. New contributory elements will need to be assimilated. Any growing preacher will change and more than once, I should think, his underground feeders. What once made a sermon alive and beautiful and fruitful will seep away. Then, if he try to preach it again, there will be no sound of the going of the winds of the spirit in its branches, only the dry rustle of dead leaves.* Much embryonic preaching is fed by stored and predigested nourishment very much as a seedling is first fed by its cotyledons. It is probably the task of a theological seminary to furnish this convenient sustenance which will carry the young preacher for a year or two, during which period he is apt to preach out of his note-books. They are dry soil from which to draw any preaching, and his people will bear with him more for the ardor of his youth than the vitality of his message. Any preacher's creative period begins when he begins, through the movements of his own mind and spirit to preach out of his contacts with life, when his faculties begin to strike through what has been given him to what he begins to find for himself. Then his preaching begins really to be alive with a power to maintain itself and make the inner and outer worlds contributory to its growth.

---

* This is why, among other things, sermons, unless quite patterned, can rarely be repeated with the first fresh power and why any man's sermons of a decade past seem strange to him. Something which gave them sap is gone.

Such preaching is rooted in the preacher's observations of life, his meditations upon it, and his sense of human needs and situations—all that and something more. (I have added "something more" to keep for the moment a door open.) There are two approaches here: One may approach religion from life or approach life from religion. Actually all religion—this sweeping statement may be risked—has, in its first free and creative stage, found its points of departure in the elements of unresolved mystery in our inner and outer worlds for which it furnished an explanation. "Religion," says Whitehead, "is what the individual does with his solitariness." It is also what he does with his wonder, his awe, and his sense of individual helplessness.

In its bright morning, it undertook to show how the perils of solitariness could be escaped, how one could live safely in a dangerous world and be in right relations with the power or powers with which a man had to reckon from birth to death—and perhaps after death.* All this was so inevitable and so natural as not even to need a name. The whole conduct of religion was tied up with the whole conduct of life. Religion was unbelievably old before anyone even named it at all. †
Then it became a system and that also was inevitable. After the system had taken some final and authoritative form the

---

* This is in substance Ward Fowler's definition of religion. Perhaps religion has over-specialized in making us safe in a dangerous world.

† The Romans did that and with their genius for organization they made a system of it—a system meant just to assume, through its rites and priesthoods, the responsibility for getting the citizens of the state safely through the perils of life, disciplining them for its duties and saving them from the consequences of their sins of omission and commission. The Romans were thereby set free for the heady enterprise of conquering and administering what world they knew or could get at. They called it "religio" because it relieved them individually of any absorbing responsibility for their souls. And religion has been just about that ever since—Western religion. (This also is Ward Fowler.)

movement was reversed and the ministers of religion thereafter approached life from the system.

Jesus used both approaches. In His divine and lonely adequacy for human need, He came from His oneness with God. In His teaching He approached religion from life. "The Sabbath," He said, "was made for man, not man for the Sabbath." "Her sins which are many are forgiven her, for she loved much." "Alas, for you experts in the law! For you load men with burdens they can hardly carry, and you will not touch them yourselves with a single finger." "Which is greater, the offering or the altar which makes the offering sacred?" These are plain and burning words; the fire which makes them still hot to the touch is Jesus' passion for religion as the servant of human need and His divine anger at whosoever and whatsoever subordinated these needs to a system. And the system broke Him on the cross.

Those who inherited from Him made in turn a system of their inheritance. That, too, was inevitable. Otherwise Christianity might have been lost in a vast and formless speculation or ended by Rome. But all this was done at great cost to the essential vitality of Christianity. Once the great creeds were drawn and subscribed to, the great Church made them her responsibility.

Thereafter the systematic structure of Christianity took awesome form and ruled the centuries. All noble preaching must be rooted in great beliefs, yes, in great doctrines; for the great doctrines themselves are deeply and timelessly rooted in the sovereign quests of the human spirit. They have behind them a history older than Christianity itself. They furnish now, and will continue to furnish, Christian preaching a substance and control without which it tends to become disarticulated cleverness.

II.

But for all that the systems have become too remote from life. Their terms are dusty with the dust of secluded library shelves and can no longer nourish vital preaching. They are vulnerable to psychology, to science, and to understandings of human nature and human history which must be taken into account. They need to be rebaptized into life. It is extremely difficult to classify contemporaneous preaching by any other test than its bearing upon life. The classification of the schools: doctrinal, expository, educational, evangelical, ethical, and the like, holds, if it holds at all, very loosely. The border lines between liberal and conservative are blurred.

In America devotional preaching done with fine literary art has almost disappeared. John Henry Jowett was the last in that rare succession and he brought his technique from England. Here and there the gift of eloquence is evident and potent. Very brilliant preaching is being done on the basis of literary criticism and its bearing upon life. This is an entirely legitimate field since literature is itself a many-sided interpretation of life with approaches whose variety, insight, and veracity the pulpit will always envy.

A younger group are acute critics of the present industrial orders but lack a definitely constructive note. Preaching is always selective; any preacher of force will create, given time enough and folk enough to draw from, a congregation which cares for and supports his ministry, though many things besides his preaching determine a church's affection for its minister. His nearest ministerial neighbor will do exactly the same thing with a preaching method and content of an entirely different order. Preaching is as pragmatic as engineering. Whatever works is good homiletics. But I think it true to say that the preaching which in the long run is most telling today is the preaching whose bearing upon life is most direct and creative. It will not always be the most popular though it should be. It will be hard to headline but it will do what preaching is meant to do and keep on doing it.

III.

Whatever portion of this gift to touch life directly and creatively a preacher possesses must be (a) fed by observation; (b) kept warmly alive by sympathetic human contacts; (c) given form and content through brooding meditation, and be vitalized by his own experience. We shall come presently to what feeds into the mind. Here is something in action behind the mind. These three: "to observe," "to feel with," "to brood," in no somber sense but as though hidden pregnancies of truth and vision were to be patiently warmed into vivid being, are the roots of preaching. Because it is and must be Christian preaching, the Way, the Truth, and the Life of Jesus Christ will give form and nature to what grows from these roots, as a planted acorn must become an oak—but neither oaks nor sermons grow in a vacuum.

Observation—there should be a better word—furnishes the preacher whatever knowledge he has of the event-current of his world. He must have two eyes (though he be no mitered bishop); eyes for passing seasons, trees against the skyline, the pageantry of clouds, fields sown or harvested, eyes for the processionals of the streets, eyes for lined faces or the smile of a child, eyes for wealth and poverty, for waste or want; eyes for the headlines in today's newspaper and eyes for what lies behind them; eyes, above all, for the folk of his own congregation. The whole of life will be there, the drama of it, the light and shadow of it, its pity and its glory.

He cannot observe detachedly. Some element of feeling must enter into every observation. Summer clouds will move

gether——." He usually quotes it in his prayer and as a reason for a thankful assurance he does not always feel. It is true in another than the fully quoted sense. In its human dimensions a small congregation is as representative as a big one.

It may—and generally does—lack the lesser inspirations: music, massed appeal, noble setting. It may—and often does—grow out of situations with which no preacher or congregation either should be asked to face: the indefensible, unforgivable, sectarian multiplication of Protestant sanctuaries maintained by a mistaken loyalty which will neither merge, readapt, nor leave to a peaceful death a church whose reason for existence is gone. No matter. A few plain folk shut in by plain walls assemble the toil, the weariness, the quests, the fidelities, the perplexities, and the confidences of our shared humanity.

They are likely to have that wisdom-about-life peculiar to those who live simple and laborious lives and a rare faculty of spiritual understanding and response. Any preacher who will preach to any congregation, no matter how small, out of life and back to life, moved by the greatness of appeal rather than their usher-counted numbers, need take little account of statistics. The unseen and enduring will fill the empty spaces, the walls of his church will open upon far horizons. What he says will accommodate its form and action to the setting, but the self-absorbing earnestness of it will be constant. What is true and right for a thousand is true and right for a hundred. Gothic arches can do no more than multiply the echoes of his voice, and pictured windows may do no more than dim the light by which he should read in the faces of those to whom he speaks the response of their spirits to what he says.

IV.

If these roots of preaching struck deep in pastoral relationship are cut, preaching will in the great majority of cases become more or less exhibition preaching. It may be brilliant but it will have little vital issue. There are, of course, preachers with an unusual faculty for college preaching and the like. They understand the mind of contemporaneous youth through much conference with it; they fall in with its moods and consequently are much in demand.

The most effective college preachers are likely to be, however, men who bring to neo-Gothic chapels some wisely selected and wisely limited aspect of what they have been preaching to their congregations at home. Others, who adorn the programs of church conferences, understand the psychology of great assembled audiences and have a flair for the main currents of popular interest. One may often perceive in such sermons or addresses their stratifications of sedimentary material and calculate the homiletic age of the layers.*

There is peril to the preacher in peripatetic preaching. Those who do it best are at their best men of a few ruling ideas out of which they make books, articles, controversies, sermons, and addresses. Their motifs are significant and vital, but their work is likely to be ingrowing. The prophet's peril and power are always in his detachment from the entanglements and responsibilities of our common life. He is free, which is power. He is responsible only to his vision—or his speculation—which is peril. Isaiah or Amos either would probably have profited by a pastorate in the Third Church in Jerusalem, where they could have tried it out on the same congregation Sabbath after Sabbath and had some reaction from the pews and even from their official boards.

The preacher's observation of the event-currents of his world and the experience-currents of his congregation, into which he has so entered through insight, imagination, and fellow-feeling that he shares them, furnishes the mother matter out of which his preaching will be shaped. Some of it will be star-dust to be shaped to shining ends, some of it will be earth-dust

---

* A friend calls them "three-deckers."

which neither by fasting nor by prayer can he bring to any but a dusty issue. Most of it, being what life and time bring to his parishioners, can be fitted into some sustaining understanding of the ways of God with men.

People need help about all such things as these; I mean about themselves and what happens to them within and without. They cannot live with any power or purpose in a welter of meaningless confusion. Their lives are woven into a web of sensitive relationships. They are happy or suffer with the happiness or suffering of others. They are caught and carried by currents over which they have so little control. If Elsworth Huntington is right, a sun-spot may eventually, through summer heat or winter cold, reach and change the climate of their souls. The flames of the corona touch our hearthstones.

They cannot always put their perplexities in clear-cut words; they need a voice to speak for them. They do not often bare their inner lives even to those they know best and trust most. Their questions are half inarticulate, but they ache with the travail of the human soul; I should think even the stars might sometimes feel the splendor and pathos of it. These are the things about which the preacher must be always thinking. They are naturally the concern of all who seek, in any region, to understand and explain ourselves and our universe. The scientist, the historian, the specialists in sociology and economics, the psychologist, and the philosopher are all the preacher's comrades and in their own fields he will need to say to each of them what Dante said to Virgil: *"Tu se' lo mio maestro, e il mio autore."*—Thou art my master and my author.

The preacher's own province should be the most human of them all. He cannot stop until he has related life to duty, goodness, destiny, and God. He may begin—if he begin with life —almost anywhere. The currents of it are always washing the walls of his church, washing through the pews, washing his own threshold. They carry incessantly what no stream save the current of human life has ever carried. They carry empty thrones and the wreckage of an economic order; yesterday some old inheritance of time was caught and swept down; today the plans of brave new building appear. They carry the last speculation of a philosopher, the last achievement of science, a book or a papal bull. They carry the flotsam and jetsam of changing orders, the headlined in journals and the fortunes of households never chronicled at all; the happiness of little children singing themselves to sleep, the questing wonder of the perplexed, shadowed faces upon whom the night has fallen deeply, radiant faces which have found an undarkened light. Just life.

V.

This is not primarily sermon stuff and nothing more; a preacher can hardly maintain that everything is ordered simply for him to preach about. His first task is not to make sermons out of it at all. His first task is to understand it. If one never sees anything save in sermonic form, he will not see it clearly. If one is always thinking in terms of "finally, brethren" and "dearly beloved, let us therefore——," he is not likely to think searchingly. A politician sees in the condition of his country only something to which to point with pride and so keep himself in office, or acidly deplore to get his opponent out of office. A statesman sees the interplay of forces and searches for principles of administration. The preacher needs the statesman's approach.

He will turn over and over in his mind whatever the life-current carries to his study threshold. He will want to know the bearings of it, will explore its sources, trace if he can in anticipation its consequences. He will not impose a pattern upon it; he will seek the hidden pattern which controls, as the laws of crystallization shape a snowflake, events, and deeds. He will be always seeking the larger pattern, the whole into which the fragmentary, being fitted, ceases to be fragmentary.

He will take care not to dictate to facts. He will sit down before them humbly and as a little child, as Huxley said a scientist should. He will be afraid of nothing save blurred vision and stopping short. He will be pitifully merciless. He will use "why" as a surgeon's probe and "how" with an engineer's technique. He will consider most the substance of things not seen and, always, he will brood and brood. His ideas will issue from his meditations, his message from his ideas. His passion, like sun-heat, will have come out of the slow focusing of the diffused till it has become a flame.

He is not asked to think unaided though he will do best in the long run to do his basal thinking for himself before he hunts for authorities and quotations. He will take counsel with the wise of all time. He will not guess when exact knowledge is available, and he will not improvise. He will try to approach disputed positions in the spirit of understanding rather than argument. He will not even dictate to his own mind; he will allow it a free creative range. Then he will bring what it reports to the test of authoritative opinion. He will be under bonds to reality; he will remember, to save himself from a too shallow realism, that there are many levels and qualities of reality. And he will never stop short or yield to the lure of the short cut. Nor avoid a conclusion because it will wreck a sermon, or shake a creed, or even leave him for a while adrift beneath a starless sky.

VI.

Preaching, no matter how deep-rooted it is in observation, in human contacts and situations, in sympathetic insight, will lack its ultimate power to convince and those overtones which make

its loveliest music if there be not in and through it some contribution of the preacher's own experience. I do not know
how to say this as it should be said. The experience element
need not be autobiography or reminiscence. It will not often
need to use "I." It will be better as it is sublimated, something
to be felt by the congregation rather than said by the preacher.
It will be warmth from hidden fires and light from an unseen
lamp. It will be the vibrant accent of certainty and through
it spirit with spirit will meet.

It should ripen through the years. It should be the shared
deposit of what the preacher himself has known and suffered
and rejoiced in. It should be high-hearted with his own victories and understandings, human with his own defeats. It
should voice the catharsis of his own repentances, the assurance of his own moral and spiritual recoveries. His own dealing with doubt should make him wise in the nurture of troubled
faith. His own dearly bought sense of the enduring should
make his preaching the shadow of a great rock in a weary land.
His own sense of the ways of God should make him a prophet,
and what he says should be vital because he has lived it.

If this were not, and sadly, too largely a preacher's dream of
what preaching should be, the vocation of preaching would be
radically changed. Age would be an asset instead of a handicap, a quiet depth of experience would outweigh clever resource, and a preacher's power would grow with the years.
Actually the market value of preaching is not thus determined.
No other vocation has of late faced so premature a dead-line.
Life does not commonly begin at forty for the preacher.

There are more defensible reasons for this than the reluctance
of a shrewd board of trustees to have an aging parson left on
their hands. A preacher needs to take great care lest the experience which should give a mellow wisdom to his preaching
bank its fires. It is now and then said of brilliant preachers,

as of coloratura sopranos, that they need only a broken heart
to make an immortal music. One may venture to doubt that.
The power of such preachers is in an élan which has never
been muted by any searching sorrow. Broken hearts are hard
to get together again. Some bruising makes them tender where
it does not make them bitter, but when life has dealt with
them too ruthlessly the note of exuberant vitality is gone; the
strings upon which a happy singing music is played are silenced.
And our time has wanted the great organ, not the vox humana.

There should be ways of making a triumphant music out of
lengthening experience, of preaching out of the depths as well
as from the heights. The secret of it should be in the preacher's own soul; in his power victoriously to gather back into
himself all that life has given or denied and, because he has
resolved it all by the grace of God into an assurance of the
supreme and enduring values, make of it a music to hearten
the pilgrims of time. If all preaching were like that it might
not crowd our churches, but its contributions to life would
never be questioned.

But the preacher's own experience, with its gains and losses,
is not the only root of vital preaching. He must be able to
share and use the experience of others. The power to do just
this is the secret of the poet, the dramatist, the novelist. Shakespeare never lived through the melancholy indecisions of Hamlet nor in all likelihood did Ann Hathaway furnish him clinical
material for the jealousy of Othello. The dramatist and the
poet may create their characters out of their dreams but they
must "dream true."

The situations the dramatist creates must resolve themselves
in consistent obedience to the forces resident within them. He
must be true to the quality and nature of Hamlet or Othello.
He is under bonds to what is architectonic in life. He thus
becomes God's understudy in the apportionment of destiny

and is in his brief hour of triumphant genius the day of judgment in action. His characters are the creation of his imagination, the courts or palaces through which they move are the baseless fabric of his vision, but once he has brought Hamlet upon the battlements of Elsinore he must thereafter deal not with a vision but with life and its issues; his imagination must be entirely obedient to what Hamlet is and must do.

It is a magic gift. Experience strengthens it up to a point. There is a point beyond which experience may dim its light and halt its action. It must transcend particular experience through its faculty to enter into universal experience. The preacher has it or else he lacks it. If he lacks it entirely, one may gravely doubt whether he was ever divinely called. If he has it, it will make his own life experience tributary to his understanding of universal experience. He will then be able to rise above his own wearinesses or disillusionments and sound that note of mastery over life without which in some modulation of it preaching is "jangled, out of tune, and harsh."

He will save his preaching from that by submitting it to the test of the sovereign words of his Christian faith. They are there: "right and wrong," "the soul," "destiny," "Christ," "God," "why" and "whence" and "whither" and "life" and "death." Nor can he escape what makes him a Christian and a preacher. He should not try to escape it. His value to his time lies just in carrying the whole of life into these regions. I should not call them so much regions as levels. He must carry everything up.

VII.

There are many ways of thinking about the electric light which illumines the table upon which this is being written. These ways belong to entirely different levels. The electrician thinks of it in terms of a science which has given a new discipline to the mind, a new empire to civilization, a new dimension to imagination and made light vocal. The engineer thinks of it in terms of water- and fuel-power, in terms of dynamos, circuits, and distributing uses. The local organization thinks of it in terms of business administration. The holding company which has built it into what is generally believed a top-heavy enterprise thinks of it in terms of high finance.

The Public Service Commission of the State of New York is just now thinking of it rather critically in terms of overcharges for gas and power. Governments, state and federal, are thinking about all such bulbs, with the vast interlocking systems behind them, in terms of their social and economic consequences. The preacher may think of it in all these ways. In fact, he should try to do just that or he will not understand what has long been, under cover, a bitterly contested front in industry and finance and which promises to be the terrain upon which a still more decisive engagement will be fought out.

Kipling and Wells have both built the structure of a new world order about transportation.* "Transportation," Kipling says, "is civilization." But so is power. If and when and as the state controls power and transportation, it will control so to speak the heart and central nervous system of the body politic. The light upon any man's desk leads through the wires, seen and unseen, which feed it straight back to such issues as these; and a preacher's meditation, if it begin with the light—which is a good place for any preacher to begin—will think it through in terms of its far-reaching social significance. There his level begins.

He will think it through also in terms of human well-being: What an abundance of light means to labor and homes and city streets, to farmhouse and barns and country roads, and all

* Kipling—*A. B. C.* Wells—*The Shape of Things to Come.*

the places where folk live or meet for toil or pleasure. He will think of light in terms of happiness and security. He will remember the tragic darknesses of the World War, cities in a fearsome gloom, unlighted ships feeling for unlighted harbors. He will thus come to measure a civilization by the abundance of its lights.

He will not be willing for any to live or work in shadows and half lights. He will see his light and what is behind and beyond it as an aspect of the moral order. What we do or leave undone in the creation and control of it will be right morally right, or wrong—morally wrong. He will test our dealings with it by the test of Christian ethics, impose upon them the high command of the Christian conscience. He will find a new meaning in the spiritual symbolism of light. He will ponder with new understanding the proclamation of the Master: "I am the light of the world."

If a light bulb will lead a preacher through many levels to the final values of life, by so much the more will the shifting lights and shadows of experience; what we gain or miss, the sense of sin and failure, all that which woven together becomes the web of our years and the texture of our souls.

The central weakness of a rotten state and a sterile religion, a great prophet once said, was that politician and priest had ceased to think in terms of human and moral values: "My people will not consider." For it is only by consideration, which might mean to hold, for perspective, the issues and interests of life against the stars; by pondering, which does mean to weigh, the issues and interests of life in the right scales, that we find out their worth, calculate their consequence, or get them into rightful proportion. Otherwise our treasures turn out valueless, the consequences of what we are or do surprise and wound us, and our lives and our society, being out of scale and balance, have no sustaining integrity.

VIII.

That is the prophet's office: to consider for the unconsidering, to set the deeds and ways of men against overarching laws and orders, to weigh profits and policies in the scales of right and wrong, to set out, as he sees some broken gleam of it, the will of God here and now. Surely if there is any way at all for an Understanding vaster than our own to reach and use our own understandings, it must be through the channels of meditative thought, asking only to know the truth, open to every suggestion of it, following to what depths and heights it can reach whatever affects life or issues out of it. There may be ways thus kept open to conclusions which have a divine validity, to an authority which dares to say "thus saith the Lord" and says it truly. Nor can one believe that if such channels were once open they are now closed.

Principal Shairp said of Newman in an often-quoted passage, which has done more to establish Newman's reputation as a preacher than some of the Cardinal's published sermons, that his look and bearing were as of one who dwelt apart. He seemed, said Shairp, to come from habitual dwelling in the unseen, to speak to others of the things he had seen and known. What a preacher brings with him out of the unseen depends a little upon what quarter of the unseen he lives in and the extent of his habitual withdrawal from the dusty ways of our common humanity. Unless, to say it again, his thought life be fed by clear seeing, warmed by sympathetic sharing, disciplined by study, controlled by reality, it may lose its major rootings in life and become an affair with speculative shadows.

With these controls such meditation is the source of all right preaching. The preacher does speak Sunday after Sunday out of his ripening wisdom-about-life. His sermons are evoked by the occasion or by his own sense of what is right to be said at any given time. He must be sensitive to suggestion. How his sermons begin, continue, and end will be due to the suggestion which calls them out. What texts he will take and when and why depend upon the association paths his homiletic mind happens to be following. He cannot escape that but he can control it. All constructive preaching follows a plan clearly or less clearly held. But no sermon is any more than some aspect of a preacher's continuing thought made for a half hour vocal.

If it be vital somewhere and somehow, some current of life has fed it; if it be creative, it will be because it has been taken by those who heard it back into life again. The capacity for such preaching as this should grow with the preacher's years. It will likely grow more simple but the range and depth of his understanding will give a mystic power to plain words. He will become for those who know and trust him a source of gratefully acknowledged strength. He will help them find the larger patterns of which their lives are a part. He will trace for them the source and issue of their dreams, help them find a road through the valley of the shadow, show them the passes in the hills before them.

If preaching, then, is the expression of the preacher's Christian wisdom-about-life; if it is, in the content of it, the revelation of the thought world in which he habitually dwells; if it takes form and direction to meet specific needs and challenges, to what needs and challenges of our own time should preaching thus matured address itself? Is there a key position upon which preaching should be brought to bear in the hope that, if that could be made subject to the Christian Way and Truth and Life, the outlying provinces would surrender with their capital? If there is it should be the grand strategy of contemporaneous preaching to advance upon that position.

CHAPTER VI

THE CHALLENGE OF SECULARISM

THE questions with which the last chapter ended were more rhetorical than precise and were unfortunate, perhaps, in their metaphors. But the most pacific of us must admit that life is a battle; that words which suggest courage and high adventure are still necessary; that the saints have hitherto found them indispensable, and that "there is no discharge in this war." It is after all a matter of causes and weapons. "We have to struggle," said St. Paul, "not with enemies of flesh and blood but with the . . . master spirits of this dark world, the spirit forces of evil on high." That fight would seem still to be on and there is, Paul held, a proper armory for this war and a Christian gear.

It is difficult to see how you can take out of our hymns, our prayers, and our preaching these ways of speaking which stand for valor and militant determination and not leave them pitiably poor. I have no such interest in seeing "Onward Christian Soldiers" so revised as to empty it of brave suggestions as I have to see it made true in fact. The pity the most sensitive should feel in singing it is not that the Christian life is a life of high courage and dauntless spiritual adventure but that the "army" is so divided, its right weapons often so ill-used and its strategy so confusedly conceived. One may have little enough sympathy for the whole "crusade" technique of the modern church and still recognize behind all our business of banners and bands something inherent in life itself which Christianity should lift to noble spiritual levels.

This bears directly upon preaching. It is practically the only way in which the fact, the force, and the strategy of organized Christianity reach the pews; or what is happening to religion reaches them either. The generality of men and women who attend "divine service" Sunday after Sunday know little more of what is going on in these regions where philosophies and critical speculation meet and engage than they know about what is going on in Mars. They do not read the books which are the actual terrain of the action, or the periodicals which report the engagements. They would not for the most part understand what is being said in any convention of the devoutly learned using the terms which are at the moment the hall-marks of religious modernity.*

They have never heard of Aldous or Julian Huxley or Joseph Wood Krutch. Jeans they might know through a wide popular interest in astronomy; Eddington and Whitehead would hardly be so much as names. If they know Walter Lippmann at all it would be through the *New York Herald Tribune*. They would know Einstein's name but no more about his new space-time than the rest of us who take it trippingly on our tongues. The old space and time are enough or too much for them. If they read our more critical and sophisticated publications they are not likely to go to church much.

The representative intelligent layman (or lay-woman) knows of religion on the whole no more than his Sunday school teachers and his minister have told or tell him. They do not know that their souls are under examination; they know only that life

---

* I heard lately a series of lectures on "The Experience of God as a Person" given by a most distinguished theologian. They were music and perfected art of speech, true insight and saturated with the unusual personality of the lecturer. But their rarefied atmosphere would have left the average layman gasping.

is difficult and that a very great deal of their religion seems to bear upon it only remotely. It is this seeming remoteness of religion from the going business of life which is just now imperiling the church, which is serious enough, and the command of religion over life, which is far more serious.

That word "command" is wrong. If religion can do no more than command life through its authority over our hopes, fears, wonders, even ignorances, its throne is always insecure. A new order of thought may displace its explanations of man and his world. A changed ethical-imperative may make of its moral sovereignty a *roi fainéant,* a "do nothing king" who is left a crowned shadow in an ancient palace while the real power of administration is in other hands. How far that is true of religion today the reader knows as well as this writer. It is certainly not as untrue as either could wish.

If religion be more and other than a command, if it be to life what the flame is to a fire, not so much an interpretation of its enterprises by a religious order as the fulfillment of thought, action, and experience to which they are destined by the Power which lifts us above our clay and makes of us living spirits, then its throne is secure. It may change its forms but never its nature—and from that it will derive its authority. Preaching has in its great epochs of renaissance and power addressed itself directly to what it then believed to be crucial in Christianity and furnished new voices for religion. It has been appeal, defense, instruction but always for its religion.

When religion has been involved in any situation which threatened the integrity or the reality of it, preaching, if it had any strategy at all, has moved upon that situation. It has done that oftener by some sure instinct than because it has been reading books on what to preach, but that is no reason why it should not use all its intelligence to understand such situations and determine its strategy for any epoch. Preaching in a critical time has no more right to spend its really vast potentiality upon minor issues than a twentieth century army, when the destiny of the state is at stake, to turn aside from its main objective and beseige an obsolete fort according to the rules of eighteenth century warfare.

I.

So we come back to these last chapter questions, and begin not with an answer but with a situation. William Pepperell Montague has put the critical situation which the church, Christianity, and religion itself face into one staggering sentence: ". . . for perhaps the first time in history we are confronted with complete secularization of the opinions, the practices and the emotions of mankind." * I would make no change in those twenty-three words except to leave out "perhaps" and suggest that "secularization" though a telling characterization does not go deep enough.

For the first time religion itself in all the historic meanings of it is opposed by an alternative system of thought strongly supported, unified, interlocking. That system, though it is far more than a system, is the joint creation of science, psychology, the studies of human culture, the critical examination of religion and its literature, and whatever else has made the modern Western mind. In so many words, it is now possible to explain the universe without the Creator-God of the creeds, morality without the Ten Commandments, personality without the soul, a sufficient life without supernatural help, and to die without the hope of immortality.

Nothing would seem to be left of what Kant thought a man could not live without—God, duty, immortality, sleep, and hope—save sleep and what hope we can find in our own wisdom and courage which is none too much. Duty as a word is left—

* *Belief Unbound*, Yale University Press, New Haven, 1930, page 1.

it being hard to do without—but only as an experimental adjustment of relationships and not the will of God. Religion, so far as the long history of it gives it any meaning, simply fades out of the picture. It may carry religious margins and survivals but they become shadows as though a living army should be attended by the ghosts of its own dead.

No one name has so far exactly characterized the situation, which is not strange. It is too complex for one thing and too new for another; new, that is, in our realization of its devastating unity. Actually it has been shaping itself since Francis Bacon foresaw and inaugurated "the entire reorganization of human thought," laid the foundations for inductive science, and, though he did not know what would come of it, proposed in substance that thereafter men should live entirely within the realm of observed and demonstrated scientific fact and law.

The cumulation of the process thus begun has come in our time and it was here before religion knew it. No wonder we do not know what to call it. There are many who do not think it worth naming since it will presently be gone; very likely they are too sanguine. It is sometimes called neo-paganism, mostly because of its morals. But paganism was always religious even if it must build temples to Venus to sanctify its passions and altars to Mars to get its wars blessed. And there was in ancient paganism at its best an untroubled joy in this earth-rooted life of ours which neo-paganism cannot recapture. That, too, is ghost-haunted.

Auguste Compte anticipated the effect of an exclusive occupation with natural phenomena upon religion and tried to make a religion to suit the situation he foresaw. He has rarely had due credit for his foresight. For an exclusive occupation with natural phenomena, that is with only the things sense can discover and reason validate, will sooner or later create its own religion though it be godless, crossless, and soulless. It must and will find an object for its loyalties, a cause for its devotions, a mystic end for its quests. Religion has always grown out of such necessities as these but Compte would not let his religion grow. He made it to plan and specification, impossibly elaborate. He built his temples, so to speak, before there was a faith for them to house, set up his altars before he had priests or a sacrifice.

Nothing remains of that either save one man's presumption and insight and a half-buried name: positivism. If that name were dug up and the dust brushed off it, a good many recent thinkers would find they are not so recent. The best name so far is "humanism" and that has already become a battle cry instead of a banner. It is an old word of many associations now taken out of its historic connotations but there is no reason why it should not be fairly descriptive of this order as made competitive to Christianity. I say "as made" competitive since there is a region in which what Christianity is or ought to be and what "humanism" may or ought to be, could meet at least with an entente cordiale. At its best this system waiting to be christened—if it live long enough to make the ceremony worth the bell and the candle—does begin, continue, and end in the closed circle of the human order.

The universe, says Maeterlink, in *Le Temple Enseveli,* is like a sealed sphere of steel. Nothing comes into it from the outside, no forces affect it save the forces already resident in it. The humanist says much the same thing of our human order; there is nothing in it save ourselves nor can anything enter it from the outside save through ourselves. We live out of what is resident in us of power or potentiality. We should, then, by the logic of humanism make the best of ourselves. The non-humanist (an infelicitous phrase) must recognize that even in this limited circle is room for a deal of plain, practical, human improvement. There are implications of really noble dignity, a challenge as of trumpets blowing down the corridors of time, in this curiously fought over and now rather discredited word.

Our humanity ought to be a challenge and not an alibi; something of implicit splendor up to which to live and not an earth-stained garment to hide our shame and weakness. A nameless Eastern teacher almost three thousand years ago said that man was God's footprint in the clay. The Western humanist is not so sure of God but he does believe our clay has taken the imprint of something beyond common earthiness which it is our task to make evident. The quarrel of Christianity with humanism is not because of what it affirms but what it ignores, and that goes deep.

Those writers who are trying to reconcile this kind of humanism and Christianity by making it synonymous with merely a fine culture are missing the mark. Christianity has often enough faced a skepticism purely negative and without a reserve to fall back upon. It has faced a speculative and arid rationalism which had no real alternative to offer for the faith it dissected and the authority it challenged. It has never before faced an opponent armed *de pied en cap*, from top to toe with alternatives for what has been central in religion since men made their first suppliant gesture through mystery to the unknown and touched—so they believed—some trailing fringe of the garment of God.

II.

There are among us far larger numbers of men and women who for the present find no support in inherited religions than the churches recognize. They are high-minded and high-purposed. The time-worn formula of secret sins, for which their doubts are a cloak, is as childish as it is unchristian. They are seeking for motives and values to carry them with courage, inner peace, and creative power through the pilgrimages of a life which is now no more for them than Carlyle's little gleam between two eternities. But even if they are "for the dark" they would not disgrace the gleam, nor bear themselves unworthily of the noble enterprise of being human.

If they should for the present get no further than making the realization of the best humanity of which we are capable the goal of their pilgrimage and out of that create an order true to their vision as far as their vision reaches, they should in that very practical endeavor, I believe, have the sympathy and help of the church. We who believe that neither the universe nor life are sealed spheres should nevertheless recognize that there are many stages in the long ascending spirals of faith and duty. We will deny no man a foothold on the terrace he has reached because, for him, the top of the road is lost in the clouds. If he should call that terrace humanism, the Christian church can offer him the supreme humanism of the teachings of Jesus.

Jesus Himself asked no more to begin with of the perplexed than that they should begin with the wounded, half-dead by the sides of life's road, the sick, the imprisoned, and the naked, and heal and free and clothe them with a love-impelled humanity. They might, He thought, learn how to love God by loving men and stand unafraid in the Day of Judgment because, with no thought of their eternal issues, they had lived merciful lives. There is an old record that certain mortally sick were healed "as they went." *Solvantur ambulando* is a wisdom the church has paid a costly price for forgetting.

For such reasons as these the religious leaders at present responsible for the creation and direction of moral motivation (using "moral" very inclusively) are at fault for not recognizing the confused estate in which we now are more frankly and, as far as the church goes, welcoming whatever will help us out of our confusion. Ralph Sockman in his *Morals of Tomorrow* is a brilliant exception to so general a statement. There are others but the pulpit as a whole still seems too remote and has very little positive help for these perplexed pilgrims. It would, one grants, be difficult for the Christian preachers to effect a rapprochement with Bertrand Russell and Aldous Huxley. But Walter Lippmann's position does offer a point of approach. The generality of the perplexed are not on the left wing nor speculatively minded. They want somewhere to go worth going to and they want to take their intellectual integrity with them.

Is there any sector on this long-entangled front where the preacher can now and here make his contribution? Yes. He can cooperate with every seeker for any wisdom-about-life which will give us any power to go on worthily and with a margin of light ahead, even if it be no more than such a short-ranged light as that with which one drives through the dark, confident only that the road is there and is built to bring him home. There is much no one preacher can do, much that can be done but slowly. The reconstruction of faith will need a vast and patient cooperation of all seekers after the good life and God, and it will need much waiting for. The time-spirit cannot be driven in a task like ours, but the task is not beyond our power.

If these last two or three pages seem to imply that the critical intelligence of England and America does not understand how vitally not only Christianity but the status of religion and the values of personality are involved in the thought movements, at once creative and iconoclastic of the time, then these pages are badly written and unpardonably presumptuous. The bearings of this latest "new learning" upon every phase of our human enterprise are being examined from every angle. We are actually in the full current of an effort to synthesize the results of more than sixty years of such insistent and fruitful intellectual activity as has not been known since the Renaissance.*

---

* The very suggestive bibliography of Ralph W. Sockman's *Morals of Tomorrow,* Harper & Brothers, New York, 1931, illustrates the range and variety of thinking and writing in just this region.

And we have never had so much out of which to make a living whole. Beneath the apparent anarchy of changing orders, beneath the dilapidations into which once proud systems have fallen, there is in action a vast organic rebuilding. The builders call to one another through the shadows from the unfinished spans and arches of it. No one can yet see the finished form it will take, though the prophet and the dreamer of time-tested dreams have built it already in their visions. There are laws which shape it, necessities of structure it cannot escape if it hopes to last. Inevitably, also, as the builders begin to meet toward the top of it where all its arches draw in and must be locked together, the ultimate realities begin to emerge and more and more demand attention, and these ultimate realities involve religion—unescapably, awesomely.

All thoughtful preaching is, of course, deeply colored by all this, but preaching has done and is doing less than it can and should to help the perplexed, who cannot go the whole road of Christian faith, to go as far as they can. It has failed to see in "humanism" a stage of the modern quest in which, without being disloyal to its own supreme persuasions, it might fall into step with those who face toward any light and lead them toward its own. For these reasons it is a pity that the whole action about humanism has been carried on in the field of controversy with so much heat, so little light, and so little finality. There are forces in action just here which have to be reckoned with and, though they may be hid by a smoke screen,* they will be still there when the smoke screen is blown away. (The creative work of Walter Marshall Horton and Henry Nelson Wieman should be recognized just here.)

---

* It is all a little like the flurry over technocracy. Here was and is something of great significance. It became merely a matter of newspaper headlines and some parental reproof from President Nicholas Murray Butler.

III.

There is still the name for what Montague describes and especially for its consequences which he himself uses; that is secularism. Secularism is not speculative and has no official creeds though it would probably approve the less devout passages of the Book of Ecclesiastes. It is a way of life difficult to define, fairly easy to diagnose, and by no means easy to cure. The symptoms of it have long been familiar. It takes many forms, some of them obscure, but they are all variants of one ruling attitude—an excessive concern with the affairs of what St. Paul called "this present world." Secularism is literally "this age-ism" and our own age has it acutely. "This present world" being complex, alluring and baffling enough, secularism may lay hold of and be concerned with any one of its interests, occupations, or satisfactions. But always as if they were ends in themselves and with nothing above or beyond them.

Life, says Abbé Dimnet, is a kind of stairway. It reaches from the sub-basement to the skylights, may be climbed up or down, or else, though the Abbé does not say this, one may spend one's life on some chosen few of its steps. It passes of necessity through all the levels of sense. It passes through action with and upon things, and whatever else—which is enough—belongs to this present world of business, politics, friendship, and enmities, plans, vocations, dreams, desires, honors, and emoluments. It is a long, long stairway; its lowest steps are below our searching; its final flights beyond our vision. The poet believes it slopes "through darkness up to God."

The merchandise of "this present world" has been catalogued with engaging completeness by John Bunyan in his description of the Town of Vanity and its famous Fair. Some new booths have been set up since Bunyan visited the Fair, mostly in Mechanics Hall, with a display of devices for speed, comfort, and

convenience in which, as a one-time tinker, he would be interested. As a very understanding tinker, he would likely recognize their bearing upon his craft and possibly conclude that they
could do no more for tinkers than ruin their trade. Otherwise
the Fair has not greatly changed in the last two hundred and
fifty years. Secularism would seem to be spending the whole
of life with a complete absorption in Vanity Fair, either as
spectator, buyer, seller, producer, consumer, or financier with
marginal occupations of banditry and racketeering.

Since this way of life with all it involves furnishes a great
variety of most engrossing interests, an increasing number of
people make it their life business. Epictetus saw this almost
two thousand years ago and said wise and lasting words about
it. The fatal fault of life, he said, was treating things as final
which are not final. "As if a man journeying home and finding
a nice inn on the road, and liking it, were to stay forever at the
inn. Man, thou hast forgotten thine object; thy journey was
not *to* this but *through* this." There are many taking inns, he
admits, and some of them he names. He does not deny their
allure and his quarrel is not with them; it is with stopping in
them when one ought to go on: "I attack the resting in them,
the not looking to the end which is beyond them." All this
is a piece with the Abbé's staircase of life.

For John Bunyan the Town of Vanity and its Fair were
simply incidents in the pilgrim way from the City of Destruction to the Celestial City. A man was saved from their dangerous allurements by getting quickly on his way. For Dimnet
they would be stages on the staircase some of whose steps are
so rotten as to allow one to fall through into the cellar, the
soundest of whose steps are meant to climb by and not to live
on. Secularism reaches from sensuality to noble intellectual
and esthetic levels. At its worst it is living in the basement;
at its best it is not reaching those fair upper chambers of life

whose windows open toward the rising sun and whose name is Peace.

The church has generally called this habit of life "worldliness" and in a phrase now grown a bit archaic used to name those given to it "worldlings." "Worldlings" neglect the means of grace, they are given to light pleasures or worse, they are of a frivolous temper. According to Bunyan they begin by drawing off their thoughts from the remembrance of God, death, and judgment to come and go on from bad to worse "until, unless a miracle of Grace prevent it, they everlastingly perish in their own deceivings." He manages a rather marvelous diagnosis of their temper and his conclusion in view of what worldlings are making of the world is still worth considering.

The church's first concern with worldiness is naturally in its effect upon church attendance and support, about which it has grave reason to be concerned. Montague's arresting sentence might be rewritten: "For the first time in Western history it is possible for entirely respectable people to leave the Christian church entirely out of their opinions, practices, and emotions and be entirely comfortable about it." The churches may be shortsighted and self-centered in thinking of all this in terms of their own authority, attendance, and finance. They probably are.

When a minister in his diagnosis of the spiritual sickness of our time brings it all back to a distressing lack of loyalty to "our church" with some subconscious reference to "my preaching," he is beginning with the symptoms and not the disease. His prescriptions are often naïve—and generally offered to the people who need them least. What is happening to the churches— significant as it is—is only an incident. What happens to life in Vanity Fair is mortal.

What happens to the world through an excessive preoccupation with its affairs uncontrolled by any vision beyond its horizons, any values beyond its material wages, and any passion save to use it for personal or party or national advantage, is also mortal. Whatever we are considering: humanism, secularism, "worldliness," or a life begun, continued, and ended within a closed circle of a this-world order with an exclusive concentration upon natural phenomena—whatever you call it, I say, there was never a stage more completely set for such a way of life and thought to show what it can do with and for the world. It has forged its own tools, laid down its own laws, taken its own high-handed course, determined masterfully its own issues—and failed at almost every point.

We have an unbelievable mastery over nature and have unified the world. And the world has been made bankrupt by past war and is obsessed by the fear of future war. Mastery over resource and magical technical skill have done nothing for us other than a fantastic distribution of wealth and a worldwide depression. We have the material and opportunity for boundless cultural wealth, and they call us the age of jazz. Our promised satisfactions elude us and the "successful type" among us "is crude, blatant, superficial, inwardly uncertain, and unhappy." Something has gone wrong. Worldliness cannot administer the world.* It is instead in a fair way to ruin the world.

IV.

It is just at this point the Christian wisdom-about-life centrally challenges and is challenged by the whole "world order." It is at every point opposed to the procedure, the ruling philosophy, the satisfactions of Vanity Fair. In plain words, it has always been at odds with this present world and proposes the sovereignty of another order. Everything which has so far been

---

* See the remarkable chapter in *The Christian Message for the World Today*—a group book—Round Table Press, Inc., New York, 1934.

said in this book bears directly or indirectly upon this situation. What has Christianity to say about "this world," what does it propose to do with it, what saving wisdom has it to offer and how and why?

Actually, if a friendly critic of Christianity with the historian's command of fact should maintain that Christianity never has known what to do with this present world, he could, I think, make a case. Christianity began in the brave dawn of it with the expectation that this "present world" would be swept as rubbish into the void when God had accomplished His purpose and chosen His elect. And this "present world" kept on. Christians began next to disentangle themselves, as far as they could and at a glorious cost of martyrdom, from the world's shadows and its stains. They had little hope of either possessing or changing it. They had a marvelous power of possessing their own souls and by the grace of God, as they confessed, getting their souls changed.

They were thereafter to live godly, righteous, and sober lives, keeping themselves unspotted from the world, "faultless children of God in the midst of a crooked and perverted age" like stars in the dark, bearers of the message of life. They had no power save their gentleness, nor any weapon save their power to suffer. By such weapons they did win the world's faith and vital regions of the world's conduct. They postponed indefinitely the last act in the drama of the world destruction, though they still expected it. And the world kept on.

Many fled it altogether with various consequences to themselves and to the world. A wise and masterful church organized their self-denials, bound them by monastic vows, and subdued their self-disciplines to her own authority affording many thereby an escape, the beauty and peace of which imagination has much magnified, very real and useful for the time but leaving the world still to be reckoned with. The church dealt with the secular powers and interests as she could, humbled their pride, subdued their ferocities, and here and there for a little got a world very much after her own heart—whose perfection imagination and regret have doubtless also magnified.

And always she dealt with the world as only a shadowed stage in a vaster pilgrimage. The church was far from humane with her foes but she did make a place for the business relationships and pleasures of humanity. She knew when to drive with an eased rein and, with a purpose and understanding for which she could not find words but only symbols, made a sacrament of the supreme events of life. In her more despondent moods she sang "Dies Iræ"—and the world kept on.

Protestantism, many maintain, changed all this for the worse. The Reformers, they say, with their ethical and doctrinal rigidities, their praise of labor and thrift, and, above all, their permission of "interest"—that magical way of putting money to work—made capitalism with all its consequences possible. They heightened and blessed aspects of life which, apparently blameless, have had an unforeseen and disastrous issue. All this is now so commonplace that our younger prophets could not get along without it. For all that it will bear some re-examination. There have been other forces in action in the last four hundred years than the social-ethic of Protestantism and more commanding. The forces which have carried the whole of Western civilization upon their fateful currents would probably have taken the direction they have no matter what Calvin or Luther or the Pope either said about the fine distinction between usury and interest.

Beyond much debate the excessive narrowing in of life to labor, thrift, and austerely disciplined character has speeded up the creation of thing wealth and the machinery for its production. Beyond any debate at all the result has been for the favored and successful the creation of an order so absorbing in its activities, so luxurious in its appointments, so abundant in its rewards as to make it a stage in the pilgrimage of life where anyone would be glad to linger and feel no call to go further.

Also for the broken and beaten it has become so disheartening a world as to make their pilgrimage a grim ordeal. The assurances of heavenly compensations, these feel, do not meet the situation; they have grown contemptuous of such assurance and even bitter over them. They have written across the front of a once proud Christian temple: "Religion is the opiate of the people." A religion which after seventeen hundred years of dominance in Western civilization has issued in what is about us today cannot be said, with every grateful allowance for what it is and has done, to have as yet dealt successfully with this world.

V.

Perhaps it was never meant to. Perhaps it is in essence, as Kirsopp Lake says, a world-denying religion. The mystery of our relationship to a world from whose dust we are formed and whose limits fret our souls is very deep. Perhaps the Christian faith which has never seen in the world anything but a fore-doomed stage upon which in a few years, otherwise inconsequential, our humanity prepares itself for its real life in eternity is right. There have always been those who believe just this.

When other solutions of our immemorial problems fail us, they recast this ancient faith into a new form * and find a grateful acceptance for it. Historically Christianity has thus been either a world-denying religion or a world-escaping religion. Those who try to make a world-saving religion out of it—save in the evangelical missionary sense—have much to work against besides the difficulty of recasting the institutions of society into

---

* So the Barthians now.

Christian molds. They have to recast a great deal of inherited Christianity itself to make a world-saving religion out of it.

And yet there have always been the wise and far-seeing who have believed not only that it could but that it must be a world-saving religion. That, they held, was implicit in it from the beginning, a task it could not escape assuming unless it was false to its Master and its own spirit. The urgency of the need they foresaw has not diminished. It has grown more pressing until today if Christianity cannot demonstrate its power in the factual redemption of the world, whatever happens to the world Christianity will be lost. The side movements (like Barthianism) are foredoomed.

Secularism is a sign of the failure of Christianity on its own front, in its first and most concrete field. It would seem after all that the present most urgent business of Christian is not to get on as quickly as may be to the Celestial City but to stay on in Vanity Fair (being in it and not of it) till he has "cleaned it up" and made it in some dim way like the Celestial City. He would thereafter more properly enjoy his heavenly rest and, perhaps, more deserve it.

If one says the first task of preaching is to oppose the wisdom of Jesus Christ to the folly of the world's entrenched system, he invites ridicule or pity or hopelessness. Perhaps the fault is not in the divine wisdom of Jesus but in our own age-long refusal to let it have its way with life and life's world. It is easy in writing a life of Jesus or preaching from His sayings to make poetry of it all—an idyll of a blue lake and its guardian hills, soon and tragically ended. The Sermon on the Mount becomes a recitative of something strangely beautiful—and hopelessly remote. How can we make a wisdom-about-life out of that? We throw out a smoke screen of "ifs" and "buts" and "whens" and "hows" and under their cover escape the searching imperative of the Christian "Way." We will love our enemies when they become more lovable, seek the Kingdom of God first when we know where and what it is, go the added mile when we have more time, and trust God for food and raiment after we have made a sufficiency of sound investments.

The reluctance or else the slowness of the Christian mind really to come to grips with the full content of Christian wisdom-about-life has been due perhaps as much to the apparent difficulty of making it workable as to the unwillingness of Christians to pay the price of living it out. Christianity has never been wanting in courage when the issue between conviction and conformity was clearly drawn. Martyrdom has never been able to break the resolution of minorities with their backs to the wall for their faith. When the price was to be paid they were always there. Whenever an individual attitude is final, whenever one can say: "Do with me what you please, I can do no other," society becomes powerless. It can torture, imprison, or kill—but it is beaten. Such as these have left a "martyr-mark at every boundary point along the boundary line" between religion and the world.

If the whole content of Christian living dealt with situations which could thus be resolved, everything would be simplified. It may sometime; it is apparently approaching such an issue now in Christian suffrage for war or peace. It may be possible to create a Christian conscience about war against which all the fallacies of a militaristic philosophy, a provocative patriotism, and even the instinct for security would be helpless. But life, unhappily, cannot generally be reduced to the plain issue of "yes" or "no." It is, to use a current phrase, an unescapable "tension" between "yes" and "no."

This way of holding the ethic-attitude of Jesus as a poetry of idealism with a power to soothe our worldly distresses and indict our worldly tempers, but in the application of it presenting difficulties to which we are not equal save when the issue is dramatically sharpened, has gone far to defeat the practical outcome of the Christian philosophy of life. It has made the Christian (I use the word spaciously) a citizen of two worlds, with no effective liaison between them. One of them is a world in which all men are sons of their Father God and brothers, in which love is the law of life, a world whose wealth is the treasure of the soul beyond the power of any moth to fret or any thief to steal. In that world sin is forgiven when it is confessed. The weary and heavy laden have a secret joy; the poor and sad are blessed. The frontiers of it are always where one is, it needs only faith to cross them and thereafter life's pilgrims, with a due measure of repentance, are secure for time and eternity.

The stupendous doctrinal structure of Christianity which makes of this present world only an interlude has been built to shelter and assure that faith. The church is its creation and effective agent. Every cathedral is in carven stone the symbol of it. Pictured windows, sacred furnishing, and hallowed liturgy confirm its truth. Priest and minister are its voices. The words of the Gospels, said or sung, fill consecrated spaces with their majesty, are broken into echoes, and die away. They also fill the souls of worshipers with their majesty—are broken into echoes, and die away.

To deny the power, beauty, service of all this is sheer blindness. To call it "escape" is to misname it. To call it "wishful thinking" is to short-circuit an understanding of elements in human nature without which it would not be human nature. To disregard what it has done for life and Western civilization is to ignore history. It is not the whole of Christianity; it is with all its implications what Christianity has become. And it would surprise the Founder of Christianity.

VI.

The real trouble is that, once he leaves the church doors, the Christian (I am still using the word inclusively) becomes again a citizen of another world. He has been for a season in the world of the idealist, the artist, the poet, a world of another order of reality "in which things are more lasting, more harmonious, and more vivid than in the world of his daily life." It is, he has felt, his true homeland—and perhaps it is. If it lay hold on him with any real power he takes away a heightened courage and a supporting faith which do tell in his life and work.

But the world which is waiting for him on the steps of the church is disconcertingly different. What gleams of infinite kindness shine through it are deeply shadowed. The spent sparrow does fall, a broken bunch of feathers. The sin absolved at the altar is waiting outside in some form of unescapable consequence. Love asks for agencies, sees the broken go by, faces the submerged and socially disinherited, and says: "What must I do, what can I do?"

This unresolved strain between the vital content of Christianity as a religion and the conditions of social life through which it must find a channel is only one aspect of a general condition which is reflected in the literature of malaise so characteristic of the last two generations. Poetry, fiction, and the more serious drama have been deeply colored by it. There is in the modern spirit a fever which cannot be cured by merely changing beds—which has been for some little time now about the only prescription offered, though there is no agreement among the doctors about the bed to which we ought next to move. Men of insight know what the poet and dramatist do not always know; that one deep rooting of our sense of frustration is in the lack of a wisdom-about-life adequate for our needs and conditions. They are realists in their social creeds but they know as teachers of religion and physicians of the soul that our real sickness cannot be cured by brilliant criticism or loose-ended programs.

It demands a reorientation of the inner life of Western civilization—at least to begin with. It needs also proper channels for that reoriented inner life to flow through. Each must create the other though whether we shall begin with the sources or the channels is just now strenuously debated. The younger men among us are all for beginning with the channels. They want a reorganization of society which will give Christianity a chance to be really Christian. Any other approaches, they say, are futile. We have tried them for centuries and got nowhere. They carry within themselves unescapable elements of self-defeat. They may be right, and they would likely protest their inability—once they have got beyond the happy period of criticism—to unite upon any program of their own as simply an unavoidable detail of the social revolution.

Beyond debate any sound progress grows out of the interaction of both elements. When, to borrow a figure from a motor car, their gears mesh, society functions smoothly. It may be far from an ideal society, but it goes. When the institution (church, government, law, industry, finance—what you please) lags too far behind the ideology of an epoch, strains appear. And since the ideology is fluid and institutions static, unyielding institutions dam up behind them an increasing pressure of demand and discontent till from time to time they break and the red current of revolution does its devastating work, after which we rebuild. Wise engineers take account of any thread of running water. Wise social and ecclesiastical engineers will do the same with what is fluid behind or beneath their own structures.

Institutional reconstruction which has no support in the very human complex of ideas, emotions, habits, and interests of very human folk also carries within itself elements of self-defeat. Your "institutionalist" very often imperils his institutions by his inelastic loyalties.* Your "experimentalist" † sees his venture fall in upon itself because he has built beyond his foundations. It is all, I suppose, a matter of timing as much as anything else. The statesman knows when to act and when to wait. Successful pioneers of brave new orders have always had a sure sense of how far their age is ready and waiting for their experiments. Otherwise they are called "heralds of the dawn" and have monuments erected to them—often on the places of their martyrdom—some centuries later.

The sounder conclusions of the student of social forms are, I believe, that institutions are the creation and deposit of life. The shapes of things are molded by the necessities of life. Life can change no faster than a man can change with it.‡ Neither can our institutions change or be changed with any hope of permanence faster than men change with them. If this be true, preaching is still left with its ancient responsibility for human nature. It must not meet those who would begin, with social forms and forces, with an "either—or." It can claim priority for Christian ideology, Christian motivation, and Christian understanding in the "both—and" enterprises of creating a Christian society.

VII.

And so we come back to the questions with which the last chapter ended. What is the strategic center of the confusion and futility of the time upon which Christian preaching might well concentrate all its force with as nearly a united command as a church divided in organization, theological tempers, and

---

* Sometimes called stubbornness with a choice of qualifying adjectives.
† Kirsopp Lake's terms.
‡ These are half-sentences, with their magic gone, from the last pages of *Anthony Adverse,* pages rich in a marvelous wisdom-about-life.

theory of advance can secure? I offer one answer: Upon the whole inadequate, "limited," and unchristian wisdom-about-life which lies behind the secularized disorder of our modern world. What has preaching to offer? The cross-empowered, inspired wisdom of Jesus Christ.

As Professor John Bennett has been saying,* when everything else is said and done Christianity stands or falls with the wisdom of Jesus about life; about its relationships and issues; about its ultimate laws and methods; about its motives and satisfactions; about its empowerments and transformations; about its faults and failures and its redemptions. Here is no time-confined wisdom. Here is a spirit and not a program, an attitude and not details, an open movement and not a closed circuit. It is preaching's task to oppose this wisdom for judgment, for correction, for guidance, and for consequence, point by point, to all the wisdom which misleads us and the worldliness which is undoing the world. Where shall it begin? Just where we are most confused, just where Christianity needs for its own sake a further demonstration of its power, just where all sorts and conditions of folks are consciously or unconsciously asking for help; in the hotly contested and still undecided field of the Christian's use of the world.

---

* In well-considered addresses in our own chapel.

CHAPTER VII

CRAFTSMEN OF THE SOUL

THE conclusions of the last chapter—that preaching can find a strategic field in correcting the disintegrating secularism of the time, and that it will begin most effectively by securing for Jesus' wisdom-about-life and its issues a regnant recognition and obedience—are not meant to limit the preacher's field. They leave a place for the evangelist, or the mystic, and for the theologian. But they do give preaching a vital and demanding situation with which to deal. They are in line with the demand of the time for realism. They associate the preacher with what is now most bravely creative.

Thinkers who are seeking a synthesis of the conclusions of science, historical criticism, and psychology are beginning to furnish him bases of support. Students of social morality, alarmed at the results of secularism, supply him ammunition. His own inherited instinct that the church and the world are essentially at odds saves him from making a sterile peace. His vision of what the Realm of God might be, not in eternity but in time, sustains and guides him toward distant horizons of Christian well-being, and his parishioners are asking for just such help.

They live in the world, work in it, make and unmake it as it makes and unmakes them. It veins their very souls. If they conceive and long for a heavenly home, it is because they have here learned the meanings of "home" beneath perishable roofs. If they lift love to the heights of the divine nature and know God best as love, it is because they have first known love in earth-born relationships and nursed its passion in their flesh. Their lives would be empty without the occupations of the world, joyless without the beauty and laughter it supplies. All the roots of their being are in its deep, strong order—deep and deep down—yet it frets them and fails to satisfy them. They cannot escape it, they will not accept it as final. What can they do?

No matter how sincerely they desire to escape the world they will carry with them, till Mother Earth takes them back, the stigmata with which she marks all her children. The body may return, in the august words of the committal service, to the earth and the spirit to God who gave it, but the spirit will carry into the presence of the Eternal the memories and qualities which earth time has engendered. How otherwise could we be ourselves? Actually every situation Christianity faces grows out of just this. Most of the militancy of the church militant and the saints is some aspect of the unresolved tension between ourselves and our world. There is no region in which wisdom-about-life is more needed.

I.

The disciplined asceticisms of the Roman church have not solved the problems, still less the petty asceticisms of evangelical Protestantism. It is not a matter of this or that amusement, it is not even faithful attendance upon the "means of grace." The much-lauded virtues of labor, thrift, and patterned moral integrity really seem sometimes to aggravate the situation. The Christian approach is, of course, the Way, the Truth, and the Life of Jesus Christ. We saw in the last chapter how easy it is to accept His attitude toward life and the exigencies of the world as a lovely poetry and a perfection be-

yond our power. For all the noble simplicity of the purely
ethical teaching of Jesus and the luminous beauty of His sureness of God and God's concern for even a sparrow spent in
flight, the practice of Christian wisdom-about-life is not simple
and not easy. Jesus Himself never said it was or would be
simple and easy. He taught in terms of universal attitudes
but He signed them all with the cross which was terribly
concrete.

He used concrete illustrations though many of their applications were for the time and the situations of those whom He
addressed. He counseled non-resistance to those for whom re-
sistance would have been suicide. He urged unworldliness upon
a simple rural folk. An inherited expectation of the imminent
end of the then world order certainly lies behind much that
He said. To take all this and disentangle it, find in it a practical control, and make of it a definite program for a world like
ours has tried every resource of Christian thought and challenged every resource of Christian character. And there is as
yet no general agreement. The first task, then, of the preacher is
to disentangle what is timeless in the wisdom of Jesus from what
was native to the time-setting of His own life and His mind.

Whatever our disagreements in that difficult and delicate task,
we will agree that He met and used the world in a happy,
human way. For thirty years He lived a craftsman's life—
unrecorded but certainly laborious. He may have been the support of a fatherless family. He knew how cool the water was
from Nazareth spring, how good bread is, the blessing of rest
and sleep. He loved the beauty of Galilean hills and saw in
wayside flowers a blossoming of His Father's love. He shared
the social habits of the time, He had a gift for friendship. There
is no sign from first to last that He refused what the simple
life of His world had to offer as long as it did not interfere
with His mission.

But always He was in spirit, purpose, deed, and vision the Master of His world through an inner detachment from it. He held it lightly—I do not mean He took it lightly. Things were incidental. There should be, He thought, enough of them to serve their purpose—enough for all His Father's children. He had a positive sense of the entire adequacy of what we now call "natural resources" for human need, though He did not conceive them as "natural resources" but as the ripening from little Palestinian fields of a Father's concern for men and women and little children.

Too many things, He said, become a peril to the possessor. They get his sense of values out of scale and lead to delusive definitions of wealth and power. Also too many of them in a few hands and not enough in most hands is indefensible; they should be shared. He did not say all this in such colorless ways as they are here said. He said them vividly with poetry and passion, and always concretely with individual application. He knew nothing about political economy; He knew the timeless essentials of human economy. And He made it both human and divine. But He held this whole order lightly. It was not an end in itself. It was a by-product of the quest for the Realm of God.* It must not dictate the conduct of life nor be allowed to set up its throne-room in the soul.

His own mission naturally detached Him from the responsibilities of the household and the business of "this world." He asked from His inner group of disciples the same detachment. He does not seem to have asked a like detachment from friends and followers of whose existence we have through the Gospels

* It cannot be justly said that Jesus thought of the creation, use, and administration of the thing-side of life as a road to the Realm of God, but this whole order is far more than a by-product of the quest for the kingdom. It might be, should be, here and now the Realm of God in action among us. His great command, "Seek ye first, etc.," is capable of a most definite application to an industrial order.

only incidental intimation. He asked of them only loyalty to His Way, His Truth, and to Him. When one puts all this together, we may conclude that Jesus' first principle—His wisdom-about-life—in this difficult matter of our relation to the world was—and is—that the values of the soul are supreme and final; everything else must be subordinate to them. He never developed the technique of the full application of this principle to even the simple social and economic life of His milieu—much less to an order so complicated as ours. He affirmed the principle, suggested the supreme motivation, indicated controlling attitudes, and left the rest to time and life and the "spirit of truth."

His second ruling principle—an utterly inadequate phrase since it is central in His life and mission—was that self-sacrificing love is life's victorious method and the supreme revelation of the divine nature in action. Here also the timeless and the situational (no such word but there should be) were entangled. Jesus had no weapons, instruments, what you please, to advance His cause save His own power to carry it through to the cross with all which is involved in that simple statement. Nor did His followers inherit any other power. In time the church did get another kind of power and used it as it did use it. Western civilization has slowly shaped instruments and institutions, then unknown, for the realization of purposes, visions, ideologies (another creaking word). Sometimes they have fulfilled, sometimes tragically defeated, the quest for the Realm of God.

But the demonstration of the centuries has been overwhelmingly on the side of His method. Whatever of enduring worth we have achieved has been through obedience to the methods and spirit of which He was the incarnation. The arresting capacity of civilization for its own impoverishment and recurrent defeat has been due to its high-handed and low-minded persistence in unchristian methods whose futility has been so often proved that one would think we should by now be wiser. "The ethical system of Jesus," says Burris Jenkins,* "is founded upon skilful insight into many of the most difficult problems of human life. . . . He pierced to the heart of present-day problems." When the church really believes that and begins to persuade the world it will begin to write a new chapter in its own history and civilization.

His third ruling principle followed: a redirection of motive and quest, "Seek ye first the Realm of God——." Here again the timeless must be disengaged from what belonged to the Jewish mind of Jesus' time and even His own mind. The scholar should know to what extent Jesus thought of the Realm of God in eschatological terms; otherwise he will miss a most important key to His mind. The preacher should know the tested conclusions of the scholar but he will not need to preach their debates. His average parishioner does not know what "eschatology" means and has only a speculative interest in the end of the world; he knows it will outlast his time and he has meanwhile more pressing interests.

Since Jesus never defined the Realm of God He must have assumed a common understanding of it between Himself and His hearers. He did illustrate it by parables, He enlarged it by suggestion, He made it actually spacious enough to include a going world whose end belongs to astronomical time and which is given us to live in and use and love and transform until, in a future we cannot calculate, it swings lifeless in its orbit.

The Realm of God is the divine order. It has a setting in time. It might be for us here and now an aspect of the enduring realized in the flux of the years. It must include the farthest star, the dimmest nebulæ on the verge of cosmic space,

* *The Christian,* April 7, 1934.

but it might also be localized in human lives and human ways on our own otherwise inconsequential planet and give to our enterprises a glory to which the stars are strange. It is the business of the preacher to try to make a little more real the divine order among us. The detail will change, the challenge endures; that and the splendor of the ideal.

II.

St. Paul will help him. He, too, has his doctrine of last things and longed to be taken up to his Lord. (He occasionally grew tired of being scourged and stoned, and Roman jails were cold and lonely.) But he saw that the folk of his churches might have to get on with the world for an indefinite period and he, the first of whom we have any record, undertook to define the technique of practical Christian living.

His "present world" was not an abstraction. It marched by with Roman legionaries, it yelled in the circus, spent its blood-lust upon dying gladiators. It loafed in the sun or misadministered an empire from a golden palace. It had a goddess for desire and worshiped her with fitting rites. It had a god for war and worshiped him also with fitting rites, and it had an "unknown god." It made slaves of half its population, fed their bodies to the carp, or used them in shameless ways. It was everything his "saints" were not, must not be. There was no merging then of the frontiers between the church and the world; the line between them was plain, sharp-edged, white with sanctity, red with blood.*

---

* The present blurring of the clean-cut line between the church and the world is an aspect of our confusion and is the motif of much discussion about the church and the world. There are two sides to it. The most assuring, I think, is that Christianity has leavened to a degree the whole Western human order. As Donald Winchester once said in substance: "Christianity is not now confined to its institutional channels; there is a vast and beneficent overflow," which would seem to be what Jesus sought.

He did not anticipate clearly a world entirely remade by Christianity though he did see a creation waiting in travail for the manifestation of the sons of God. He did in the concluding passages of his letters go into great detail as to Christian attitudes and duties. Those chapters are epochal for they are first visions of Christianity entering the world through the doors of daily life and social relationship.

He did lay down one governing principle: "Be not conformed to this world, but be ye transformed by the renewing of your mind." A Christian, he said, must not fall in with the "scheme" of the "world" which then flowed through the streets of Corinth or Rome. He must not allow the hot metal of a Christian passion for the Realm of God to cool and harden in such molds, they were not fit for it. We are here, he said, to be transformed in mind and spirit and through such transformation to discover the will of God. He would have approved Abbé Dimnet's figure: Christianity is going up stairs.

St. Paul left to the future leaders and teachers of the churches the full development of this. He did not need to say that transformed minds and lives will in time transform the world. He did not need to say that the world furnishes the conditions through which or in reaction to which the transformation is achieved. He was only concerned that it should be sought and accomplished. He had no program; he had only a creative passion. He knew that the key to the transformation was the "mind of Christ" lived out in Rome or Corinth or cities still to be built in undiscovered lands. We know now, as he could not know, the long sequence of action and reaction between the Christian mind and way and their always changing environment.

Molten dreams, said Anthony Adverse, must be poured into the mold of life. Almost every phase of our this-world conditioned life is a form into which some molten dream or other can be poured. Nor does this contradict St. Paul. For the molds themselves are plastic—the dreams can give them shape —and more than shape; they can change their quality and make of the forms of things and sense a vehicle for the qualities of the soul. It is only when we choose molds wrong for our molten dreams to pour into or refuse to let the dream recast the mold that we begin to conform.

On the other hand, as Adverse saw, new dreams must issue out of old molds. Anthony's creator made him, after much searching, some of it tragic and some of it unseemly, find a simple world of beauty, labor, love, and considerate relationship which was a good mold for the hot metal of his dreaming, seeking soul to flow into. "This is good mold here. . . . All the shapes of things I see about me are suitable, made beautiful by the sweet necessities of daily human use. Such images are the stuff out of which good dreams take shape—to be recast. For it is always the dream into the mold and out of the mold the dream again."

III.

Substitute the mind of Christ, the Christian ideal, the Realm of God for Anthony Adverse's molten dreams and you have the Christian wisdom-about-life, the Christian interpretation of history, the secret of the Christian use, and the Christian transcendence of the world. The preacher can preach that with passion and power. We can be very concrete and even very banal; business is only an aspect of the general business of life; banks and finance are only tools, wise or otherwise devices for human well-being. The "transformation" of a wheat field (Paul might have said) is bread and the transformation of bread health and strength, and the transformation of health and strength are what we do with them. What we do with them is what we and our world become, what we and our world become is a stage in the eternal process.

Preaching thus directed, if it be wise and resourceful, may help people to see their relation to the world in a very true light (there are certainly texts enough) and suggest a new range of values which will turn out, no matter what they are called to begin with, to be Christian. Above all, such preaching in redirecting motivation may release transforming forces. We preachers talk a good deal about the gospel supplying new motives. And so it does. But quite as much or more (examine the method of Jesus) it gives a new direction to old motives. The motives are always there; the longing for happiness, well-being, security, fulness of life. Loyalties are always here, asking for objects of devotion. The power to create is always here, asking to create. Mind-hunger for truth, emotion-hunger, the nostalgia of the spirit—these in some form or another are always in action. They have been perverted, thwarted, stupidly used, and tragically misdirected. The splendor and power of them have been often enough wasted upon the cellar and back-stairs of life. They have made men dreadfully wrong in the greedy or criminal use of them. They have been too often as water poured out upon sand.

When motives of splendid potentiality are wasted upon what is not great enough for them, cannot express the hidden wonder of them, they make everything inside and outside human life difficult or wrong. The inconsequential gets magnified. Satisfactions—because they do not satisfy—become Dead Sea apples; their bitter dust poisons the soul. One can find behind almost any depressing aspect of contemporaneous life a motivation which, if it could have been guided toward the right expression, would have made another civilization. The reckless restlessness, the ominous disquietude of our time are the protest of a vast inner force against the all too narrow channels in which we seek to confine it and the inadequate issues to which we carry it. It is as though the St. Lawrence, though it drain half a continent, could never find the sea.

IV.

It is the task, among other things, of Christian preaching to indicate the right channels for this force of motivation, to purge and exalt it. It is the task of Christian society to make of itself these channels. Critics say bitter things about nationalism though they recognize at the same time that the patriot finds in his state a satisfaction for his baffled longing for power and importance. And they sometimes score him—almost like a fishwife with an academic vocabulary—for swelling with pride when he sings "MY Country, 'Tis of Thee." The motive has in it possible elements of sacrificial nobility and his emotion as he sings is sincere, though he may not know all the verses. There might be a way of making a sacrament of his patriotism and holding up before him the ideal of a nation upon which he could worthily lavish his wealth of affection and loyalty.

What a man will die for has in it some aspect of what is supreme. He may die for a futile, foolish cause but he does not die as the fool dies. Dust made pregnant by the blood of men who have died for that dust is thereafter sacred. Why not use a passion like that instead of calling it a "lust"?

The only way, apparently, in which this can be done is by the creation of a new range of values. This also is commonplace but the one thing an utterly idealistic Christianity may forget—has forgotten—is that these values cannot be detached from the going concern of life. They must be somehow associated with the tasks and tools, the experiences, the institutions which supply the setting and furnish the occupations and constitute the interests of this present life and this present world. The soul does not grow in a vacuum. It grows by making out of itself, in relation to what it is planted in, a world to which it is native, in which it may express some hidden quality, or else be fed with some sustenance for which it hungers.

Robert Browning knew that; "God plants us," he said, "where we grow," and any attempt so to transplant a life as to save it from the peril of growing where it has been planted is self-defeating. The peril is part of the condition of growth and can only be escaped by growing through it into the brave maturing of what is most nobly native to the soul. To this motif he set all the music of his finest song. It is often enough a somewhat discordant music as though he were in too great haste to compose and did not carefully enough revise his score but it is a brave and veracious music, a marching music for life.

This has not been the dominant motif of Christian poetry, especially its hymns. They contemplate the felicities of the transplanted life with not so much consideration as would be wise of how we shall employ our present setting not as a forcing bed but to get a sturdy growth of soul worth transplanting. Every analogy seems to indicate that we shall win our souls not by escaping the world but by choosing the aspects of it in which we should like enduringly to live and at our best. We get a soul for music by living in the world of music which musicians have created. I do not know with what strings the harps of heaven are strung but the violins which make audible the stormy music of the symphony Eroici are strung with catgut, their vibrations are carried by earth air waves and heard through the mystic mechanism of the ear. How can we get a soul for music otherwise?

Nor can we in any other way get a soul for art; pigments,

brushes, canvases, and the artist's finger—are they not all earth-stuff with a power to create a world which is not of earth at all? Whence is our soul for beauty save from the refraction of light waves through the dust of the stratosphere which is said to make the sky cerulean, or through raindrops or the wind-borne banner of cumulus clouds, from the pageantry of earth and the perfume of wayside growths which blossom but to die; from all these and our own power to see them as something lovely and transformed, radiant aspects of timeless reality, near and dear approaches to an infinite love as Jesus saw them.

All our goodness is in some way an issue of our earth-born sense-conditioned lives. Chastity is a way of using sense; honesty a way of using facts and things; justice a way of living with others and adjusting the strains and competitions of such relationship, and so on through all the seven cardinal virtues. They are our right way with men and our world and ourselves, and because they are just this they become our right way with God. Out of these actions and reactions our souls emerge. They may, they do thus take on a quality which will not end when the fields of time from which we have a power to reap enduring harvests are no more. What sense has given us may endure when sense is gone. Here it would seem is the true meaning of the "spiritual"; the most necessary and most vaguely used word in the preacher's vocabulary.* What we have become may be immortally right for another setting. But we have gained it by the ministries of earth and time experience; and if this is worldliness make the most of it.

---

* No word we use is in greater need of interpretation. The ghost of its old, old meanings as an airy guest within the body still haunts all the definitions of it. The spiritual in *us*, at least, might be a way of so taking and transforming our earth-contained lives through love and good-ness as to win for them a quality of being fit for the eternal. (I do not mean "conditional immortality.") But if it be that, it will in action give to all it shares and uses a "spiritual" quality.

V.

Religion has always had its sacraments, outward and evident signs of an inner and spiritual reality. They began, it may be, in what is now for us magic, though they were no magic for those who first sat at a table which the dead or the gods could share. Even in the dim dawn of it sacramentarians believed that material things could have a spiritual use and body-forth another order of reality. The Christian church took this belief over and continued it in her own uses. She gave to bread and wine, devoutly taken, a power to save the soul and presently enshrined them, righly consecrated, as the broken body and shed blood of her Lord and the real presence of God. She made a sacrament of priesthood for the priest and of marriage for the householder. She made thus of the pilgrimage of life a mystic procession attended by the divine and with immortal issues. And she stopped too soon.

For if bread and wine can be sacraments upon the altar, they may be sacraments—visible evidences of the Unseen—in the wheat fields and the vineyards. Then the service of the field and the vineyard may become as sacred as the service of the altar. The miller who grinds the grain and the baker who makes the bread belong—if we but believed it—to the sacerdotal succession. If marriage is a sacrament so also may building walls and a roof be a sacrament or laying a threshold for the bride to be lifted over. We are ready now for another definition of what Montague described. The peril of secularism is not in its occupations. It is in losing entirely in the conduct of these operations our confidence in any reality but the reality of sense-known things scientifically tested and approved. It is an inadequate realism.

This is often called the scientific age. The age may be scientific but its folk are not scientifically minded. If we were we would have some glimmering sense of the relation between cause and effect. We would think analytically, we would test our conclusions, and we would not be blown about by hot gusts of mass passion. We are actually quite the opposite. We misapply our skepticisms and magnify our credulities. If we had been scientifically minded we would not be in our present mess. We do try to be realistically minded and go wrong there also. We more or less see the things under our noses but miss, if we do not take care, the realities of which they are only the vehicle. There is no way out of this inadequate realism save through it to what lies beyond it. There is no religious value in any order in which facts are ignored, loosely held, made subordinate to this or that interest no matter how supposedly sacred. The church has done enough of that and paid a great price for it.

But facts may be followed into another range of reality for which the factual world supplies an indispensable threshold, of which it is indeed the revelation. All sensible things may be so used as to become outward and evident signs of an inner and spiritual grace and become hallowed in so being used. This I take to be the sacramental view of life. It need not mean the same thing for different minds and temperaments, still less does it need to be tied up with any religious doctrine. Nor does the name itself greatly matter. It is a way of taking and using every aspect of sense and stuff so as to make them the conveyors of values for a perfected humanity and human order and finding in them always the sense of "something still more deeply interfused." It does not greatly matter what we call it so long as we do it.

This approach should do much toward not only making a Christian at home in his world with no sense of strain; it might supply the reconciling formula between the spiritual and the material. Nobly followed it would transform every earthly task. It would transfigure our whole industrial and economic order, making of business a holy enterprise and not a greedy game. It would create right human relationships between groups who ought to be comrades but whose contacts are now seamed with hate and knife-edged with violence.

Business might thus become a setting in which to develop a rich many-sided personality compared with which pulpit and desk and book-created personalities would be colorless—if only business were a sacrament, the actual use of stuff and process for the values of the soul. This view and way of life would save the senses—all of them—from the reproach of the ascetic or the abuse of the sensualist. They would be windows for beauty to shine through and portals for music and dear voices to enter and strings to be played upon. But always for what is above and beyond them. We should then be kind to Mother Earth and add to every landscape the beauty of reverent human use, of long and loving habitation.

John Ruskin recognized clearly sixty years ago that what we are doing to the earth may be a register of what we are doing to our souls, a scathing judgment upon our social methods and an almost infallible test of our political economy. He approached the whole secular life of his time from the judgment-base of beauty and human well-being and found it thereby condemned, and his judgment was in turn disregarded —he was only an art critic with a magic and erratic pen. But beauty, the wise have always known, sits as an equal with truth and goodness upon the thrones of judgment. The psalmist knew long before Ruskin that unless the beauty of the Lord our God crown the work of our hands they cannot be established.

It has taken us two generations to see the connection be-

tween once clear streams changed to sewers or yellow with
the eroded soil of deforested hills and the short-sighted political economy which created the economic man, laissez-faire, the
devil-take-the-hindmost. Yet the connection was always there
along with the economic stupidity which refused to change
the system and the passion for terribly costly acquisition which
drove the whole ill-geared and unbelievably wasteful system.
As long as only the poet, the artist-dreamer, the prophet, or
even the Master saw it, we did little about it. Now that the
system has brought us to the edge of an economic abyss we are
beginning a little to change it and mend what we have broken.
"Unto this last" may yet be quite orthodox political economy.
If we do make a regenerated economy and sociology roads to
the Realm of God we shall find a shining company waiting at
the end of those roads to say, "Long ago we told you."

The sacramental view of life has a great contribution to make
in all these regions. It will use things, all things—even a tree
or a clod of earth—reverently, lovingly, and as some dim setting out of the spiritual. "The world," said Emerson, "pro-
ceeds from the same spirit as the body of a man . . . a projection of God into the unconscious." If we could only handle
this projection of God as the priest his chalice upon the altar,
we ourselves would gain a sense of the mystic significance of
life and love and labor now too largely wanting. We would
be realists in dealing with facts and forces but we should be
always gaining a surer sense of what is really real.

Most of us have moments in which we see, in some clear
light, the vaster meanings of life, feel that we have for a
fugitive hour known what it is to live entirely unfettered by
space or time. Such experience might be the veracious anticipation of a far more common experience, not mystic, for few
of us are mystic, but the result of a happy correspondence
between the life within and the world without.

VI.

Those religious teachers who are not thinking most clearly about a creative Christian relation to the world are more and more taking this line. If they are logical they must make a larger place in the good life for a range of satisfactions, very simple, generally accessible, and blessedly rewarding, which our heated time has to its cost overlooked. Happiness is far more dependent upon our faculties of appreciation than our power to get and keep an engrossing variety of things. Any sensible man knows all the qualifications of this wisdom-about-life.

Economic security is indispensable, so is congenial and creative occupation, so are health and homes which are not merely human warrens in slum streets or lonely farmhouses falling into decay. It is not safe or Christian to ask men and women to live in smoke-darkened ugliness or be lost in somber mass inconsequence. We have no right to preach the gospel of simple happiness without at the same time making ourselves desperately unhappy till we have got all that changed. Every preacher has parishioners who ought to throw whatever Polly-anna preaching he indulges in back into his face.

But we can go too far the other way. The general economic concern of rural New York ministers is just now a higher price for milk. They are not preaching the esthetics of rural life though Cornell is teaching them. Anyone who preaches the beauty of country life in the Finger Lakes region to farmers who are selling milk for less than cost, and throwing in their own laborious lives, will not get an appreciative hearing. They want something more from their herds than the moral rewards of the "service motive."

Nevertheless we shall never populate rural America with contented, happy folk until farming becomes a life as well as a business, whose final compensations are comradeship with the wonder of growth and ripening, the steadfast ways of the good earth and the overtones of light and beauty which make a music for the quiet sequence of the seasons. Account books balanced in red will drain our countrysides of course or else eventually dye them with another red than ink, but without the appreciation of all the values of a life hauntingly near to old, old earth-born and earth-ripened things, farming will lack the ties which bind humanity to the soil not in drudgery but in freedom. A preacher may say that even to folk embittered by the price of hogs and cotton, wheat and milk.

This is true of every calling. The wages of life are in the end so simple that only poets seem able to invest them with a golden glow. They are not, the preacher thinks, dramatic enough for sermons. Why should he preach about quiet ways of happiness, the holy use of every sense (he inherits the habit of calling them carnal satisfactions), contentment without distinction and making the good, human, here-and-now most of everything which combines to give us more happiness than we commonly get, when there are so many dramatic, controversial, "headliner" things to preach about? There is little either to help or encourage the preacher to do that.

His world is busy about its depressions. His religious journals are usually starting him on a crusade, or getting someone to tell him what the church ought to do in the next four years. The younger major prophets are preaching about the coming social revolution and debating whether they ought to fight in it or just be stretcher-bearers. (The church has had considerable experience in being a stretcher-bearer.) There are few books on the art of happiness. Religion distrusts it. It is not commonly taught in theological seminaries.

I do not say we have any right to a thoughtless happiness or to refuse through some sheltered personal good fortune to share the travail of the world. Only that life ought always to be carried as far in the direction of happiness as possible. That the art of it should be explored and taught. That even in a world like ours it is not remote, impossible. That if we are happy only at intervals the shadows are then lifted. That there is a way of finding happiness on the edge of peril.

I remember an evening in the Argonne when for a strange hour the guns were entirely silent and three of us who had long known and loved each other sat before a little fire on a shattered hearthstone in a ruined house. We seized the hour and were happy. It was a tremulous happiness at the mercy of the unforeseen, but it was real, and when the awakened guns broke its peace we thanked God we had had that hour.

The art of happiness is partly to seize it, if only for its brief hour. It is more entirely in the training of appreciation; a way of opening eye-gate, ear-gate, heart-gate, mind-gate, soul-gate to what beyond the outer show of things may come in and possess our lives, but always through these gates and all these gates. How all this opens upon art, too remote one grants you for too many, and literature blessedly accessible and kind ways of living together and good ways of living with oneself and how the Christian faith should sustain and complete it all, a preacher must find out for himself before he can say it to others.

Here his thinking may center itself, from this center follow many branching paths but they must always come back to life again. No one can say that such preaching will be easy. It is not easy to say things about life which are not either the commonplace of all experience or else just words—true enough but strangely far from the haunting, elusive mystery of life itself. Nor unless the preacher has unusual gifts of art and insight will it be popular enough to interrupt traffic.

But it will have a quiet, constant strength, it will never lack a theme, and it might if there were enough of it do much to steady our unbalanced world. For we miss the goodness of life through our restless passions and our grandiose enterprises. We fear its simplicities and so we miss its splendor. The howling dervishes of the stock exchange, the press, the stump—and even sometimes the pulpit—the grave-faced simalcura of statesmen with their policies of pride and power and death, our heat and our haste—what are they all but our footless quest for life—when all the while the peace and beauty of it wait always for us to build roads for them, open the door and let them come in.

> " 'Tis life whereof our nerves are scant,
> More life and fuller than we want,
> Oh, life not death for which we pant."

For those who seek it thus there sounds across the vanished years the words of the Keeper of its secret: "I am come that ye might have life and have it abundantly." For what end beyond this our Mother Earth has been shaped out of the "infinite mystery" and fashioned for our sunlit and gracious habitation, we do not know. Nor do we know why we ourselves are pilgrims down the roads of time if not for just this: that by the grace of God we should so use earth and time with all our force to keep our rendezvous with life, the life the Master came to give us.

CHAPTER VIII

BASE LINES

OUR more resourceful universities now offer first-year courses in "orientation." Since freshmen do not commonly know what "orientation" means they are more likely to elect through curiosity than intelligence and be disappointed when they find that an "orientation course" is only a member of the faculty trying to tell them what education is all about, and how they may steer a reasonably safe course through perilous academic seas and come to harbor with a diploma and a cargo of merchandisable learning.

The freshman's grandfather—if he went to college—needed little advice about electives; there was nothing to elect. His courses were there waiting for him; good, stiff courses in the classics and mathematics, dry-as-dust history, compulsory chapel, and compulsory church. They furnished the orientation.

He was made and disciplined by a system which had, since Abelard left the cloister schools of Notre Dame and led the youth of Europe across the "little bridge" into the narrow, twisting streets of old Paris to sit on straw, go hungry, use their minds, and become the University of Paris, been controlled by a unified conception of education.

There are still among us those who believe that this system created a type of mind which has given to the Western world for eight hundred years whatever intellectual distinction it has possessed, but education has taken another line. A modern university offers youth a bewildering variety of alternatives and, since there is no longer any compelling unity in the system, the student must build through his own unity of insight and purpose and out of all the material his university offers him his own right structure of education. Considering what he is and what his world is, this is perhaps the truer educational method.

For the university is, after all, only a highly specialized cross-section of its world. We live in an elective order. The old compulsory courses are undone, the only authority left seems to be the authority of the mass or the dictator—a tragic alternative. The individual has never in Western history seemed to count for so little or been so free from the moral and religious disciplines which have hitherto secured for society its real unity; and yet the right kind of individualism has never, by a curious paradox, been so strategically important.

The world, like the university, is disorientated. For the present, at least, the first thing the individual must do is to orient himself. This will at least save him from personal shipwreck; it may through some slow and massive reorientation, thus secured, of the soul of society, recover for civilization itself a measure of unity, peace, and creative power.

I.

Orientation seems to have been religion's word before it was the navigator's word or the university's word. It has sunrise and sun-worship behind it. The sun-worshiper built his temples to meet the dawn and buried his dead to rise with the morning sun upon their transfigured faces. Christianity inherited all this and had, besides, its own reasons for worshiping toward the east: the devout thus faced toward the hill of the cross and the sepulcher in the garden. How church architecture, liturgies, and practices have been controlled by such orientation is an affair for the specialist. The preacher should know that religion is the orientation of the soul. It should face us toward moral and spiritual regnancies, furnish the base lines of character, conduct, and faith, and so bring a disoriented world into obedience to those truths and laws which alone can save us from anarchy.

There are meridional lines for business, government, society, if we can only trace them and are willing to find our ways by them. We call them laws of the social, economic, or moral order; or right and wrong, or the enduring values, or the will of God. The Christian calls them the Way, the Truth, and the Life of Jesus Christ. Whatever freedom and power we possess come through our obedience to their command. They are the framework of whatever order now rules among us, they are:

> ". . . a light to guide, a rod
> To check the erring and reprove."

Through them our souls, like the "most ancient heavens," are fresh and strong, and without them our human order would fall in upon itself.

There is now an almost desperate need for a new assertion of them. The release of forces new to human experience, the creation of a machinery we have not yet learned how to master have left us inwardly baffled. Society does no more than magnify and project and give mass power to whatever is resident—or wanting—in the individual. Our social action, therefore, is a picture of what is going on inside us cast on a great screen. The picture shows us, with no sure knowledge of what we ought to spend ourselves for, or upon what we should lavish our wealth of loyalty and desire, our divine capacity to lose ourselves for a cause, a banner, or a dream.

A succession of ends and values has come and gone. With the dawn of the century we were idealizing progress. We identified it with applied science, an increase for the favored of comforts and luxuries, popular education, and "triumphant democracy." It was, we were told, an evidence of God's particular concern for the Anglo-Saxon and the "one far-off divine event" toward which creation had been moving. The gospel of progress was whole-heartedly accepted and furnished those who profited by it about all the gospel they needed. When the gospel of progress perished in the holocaust of the World War it left the younger generation of idealists no gospel at all. Which is one key to their post-war attitudes.

For a hectic decade in America the maintenance and increase of prosperity oriented business, politics, and even religion. We wrote a new answer to an old catechism. The chief end of man is to glorify prosperity and enjoy it forever. "Recovery" of late has supplied an elusive orientation. There have been stars of lesser magnitude in our governing galaxies. These are what you please: self-cultivation, esthetic and other satisfactions less praiseworthy, and always nationalism with its train of pride, patriotism, its sense of power, and its militant willingness to prove its power against all comers.

None of these have been able to bring creative order to our affairs. They have, on the contrary, made them still more confused. They have introduced strains where we need a reconciling wholeness. They have divided us against our neighbors and ourselves. Somewhere back of it all there is the unresolved play of forces which have long been in action. Our Western civilization, says Plimpton Adams, shifted its center of control during the late Middle Ages from the contemplative life to the life of action and possession. "Neither to Greek philosophy nor to Christianity did it appear that the vocation of man consisted in the rational control over life and over nature's energies in order to satisfy human desires. For . . . the ancient and medieval worlds, man's essential vocation was *contemplation,** the possession, in thought or in feeling, of these eternal and absolute perplexities and forms which are both the ultimately real and the ultimately valuable."†

The glory of the past bears out Dr. Adams's conclusions. The Hebrew found the chief end of life in the contemplation of the glory and the goodness of God. The Greek gave lovely form to his thought of the true and good and his vision of the beautiful. His literature, his philosophy, and the perfect beauty of his sculptured temples were the creation of his inner life. They were not for anyone to possess; they were only to make evident what he had seen with the eye of the soul.

Rome was not given to the contemplative life but it came back again, much changed, with Christianity, and kindled on every altar the always burning lamp of the real Presence. For Dante the ultimate felicity of the highest heaven was the beatific vision. The *Divine Comedy* was, Carlyle said, the voice of twelve silent centuries. It was more than that; it was the last great expression of the ideal of the contemplative life.

Then the center shifted. The highly explosive energy of the West took its appointed line. The will to action, possession, and power has motivated Western civilization for seven hundred years. It has written a history which the most hostile critics would acknowledge to have been marvelously creative, which the most tolerant critics could not successfully maintain

---

* Italics the author's.
† *Idealism and the Modern Age,* George Plimpton Adams, Yale University Press, New Haven, 1919.

to have been characterized by any serene contemplation of the true, the beautiful, and the good, nor by the quest for the beatific vision either. We have lately had some exercise in contemplating the consequences of what we have been doing but that can hardly be called edifying. Even religion has changed its own center in obedience to forces which have been too strong for it.

II.

All this is an overstatement of course. The old orientations of life have held, do hold. Otherwise we should have fallen into utter confusion. Our tasks, as Emerson said, are still our life-preservers. Family life with all its seen and unseen filaments still supplies the major meanings of life to most normal folk. Duty and loyalty retain, not too much diminished, their ancient powers of command. Dreams of station and accomplishment are as enduring as human nature. They change their form a little but never relinquish their empire. Such things as these and the sheer gravitation of life for which there is no name at all * hold us to our stations and our tasks and give to life a continuing identity.

In spite of all this there is among us a dissolving of inherited controls in church and state. We cannot easily hold together the near and necessary things which we have been considering if religion loses its assuring force, morality its sanction, and the state is no longer worth our loyalty; still less if we distrust our own souls and consider them no more than figments of the imagination entertained by functioning organisms controlled by the ductless glands. We see along every

---

* Bergson's *"élan vital,"* "the life force," the will and passion to live.

horizon signs of what may happen to a society for which controls hitherto adequate have begun to lose their validity, whose pole-star is cloud-hidden. It has not been reassuring.

The church and its ministry should hold a strategic place in a world like that. Russia, as Maurice Hindus says, is showing us that a state *can* be reoriented without them, and a type of human nature new to Western civilization built upon their ruins. The church for its own salvation, and still more for the salvation of our society, should seek to avoid that issue. Unless it has a power to bring its world into a Christian orientation, it will itself be lost and the preacher, who will make any positive contribution to that exigent task, must first of all orient himself.

A perplexed ministry can do little more than add its own uncertainties to the general welter. I do not say the Protestant minister (of the Catholic priest I do not dare to speak), if he be at all sensitive to the thought-currents of the time, can just now recover the mystic and dogmatic certainties of inherited orthodoxy. The frame in which these closely articulated confidences were contained is broken; earth and sky and time and space are changed. But he must be sure of something and something sovereign.

Some measure of the resourceful brilliancy of contemporaneous preaching is due, curiously enough, to its lack of positive content. It attracts the contemporaneous mind but renders it little constructive service.* A good deal of the appeal of this kind of preaching has been in its faculty of mordant criticism. But man does not live by criticism alone, he needs some certainties besides the certainty that most things are wrong. The

---

* I am inclined to think it does it positive harm through the lack in such preaching of a constructive message.

things a preacher may be sure of need not reach to our last horizon's rim nor include the predeterminate councils of God, but unless he has heard for himself

> "Authentic tidings of invisible things
>   Of ebb and flow, and ever-during power;
>   And central peace, subsisting at the
>   Heart of endless agitation"

he cannot convey them to others. He will have no gospel, no good news for a time which needs more than anything else good news of meanings and stabilities in life beyond the power of any storm to shake.

It is the strategic task of preaching, if it can do no more, to furnish an embattled age the Christian base lines from which it can make its advance. They may be to begin with no more than moral and spiritual attitudes, no more than an orientation of the mind and the will and a redirection of motive, but they will reveal the lines down which we are to go, if the Realm of God is to be more than a dream.

The church can, the writer believes, do little more in this generation than secure a dominant Christian-mindedness toward the facts and forces of our world. It will be fortunate if it does so much as that. It might not be the church's province, even if society were far more plastic to Christian idealism than it is, to submit detailed plans and specifications for the rebuilding of society. He doubts if the Realm of God can ever be reduced to blueprints! Society is always essentially a growth. Even if its mechanics be radically changed, they come to little till some slow transformation of the human element overtakes and makes of them a living organism.

The church, having created the attitude, must always leave detail to the specialist. Christian economics is the province of the Christian economist and so with finance and politics.

There must be an element of trial and error in all our advance. The strategic consideration is the lines up which we move, the basal attitudes from which we take our departure. We may not agree in our cataloguing of them but these do seem plain and imperative Christian attitudes preaching should seek to establish.

III.

The first base line should be a recovery of the recognition of the power and responsibility of the individual. We can at least begin with ourselves. There is within and around every life, not broken beyond repair, a region of individual power and responsibility by no means insignificant. For each one of us that is our kingdom which we can administer and administer nobly. Its frontiers march with the frontiers of other lives. Our administration of it involves the well-being of others. It affects business or professional life and the integrity of the state. We may even govern it as our personal province in the Realm of God.

The wise have always believed it the strategic region upon whose right administration everything else human depends. The whole disposition of the time is to underestimate its significance though now and then a voice is raised in protest. "There are no powers irresistibly at work," says Sir Herbert Samuel,* "like destiny in a Greek tragedy, sweeping mankind this way and that, forces against which effort is futile and hope is vain. Look closely and you will see that there is nothing there but your decisions and mine, your actions and mine, and the decisions and actions of millions of others like you and me. We ourselves are the 'Spirit of the Age.'"

The most insignificant life has unsuspected power for good

---

* *The Contemporary Review* for February, 1934.

or evil. There is undreamt-of possibility in the conjoined action of a multitude of common people who would do no
more than administer the little regions of their own lives in
an entirely Christian way. They are, individually, the ad-
ministrators of very little kingdoms and soon reach the frontiers of the power to do and to be. But a glacier flows, they
say, through nothing more than gravitation and the movements of its molecules of water which have, when liquid, a
very little space within the crystal walls imprisoning them down
which to flow toward the sea before they freeze again. And
a moving glacier can channel the hills.

Men of large influence and responsibility, strategically placed,
affect wide areas of our common life. They determine,
through their administration of their own lives, the well-being
or the misery of multitudes of men and women whom they
never saw and who never saw them. These are cold, colorless
words but what they stand for is anything but cold and colorless. Great regions of contemporaneous business are demonstrations of just this.

Every major investigation of American finance (particularly)
has for a long generation laid bare shameful, festering situations which have been nothing less than the creation of perverted individual character. They have involved "headline"
personalities. Such men were apparently operating in fields
of national policy, world politics, or in fields of industry and
finance with which the administration of their own personal
lives had little to do. Actually they were not; they were pro-
jecting into diplomacy, international relations, finance and industry their own master motivations and the disorder of their
own souls.

They had been drunk with pride of power and greed for
gain; they had been unteachable; they had been inhospitable
to ideals and methods which challenged their enormous self-

sufficiency. They have had no inner control adequate to the power in their capable and rapacious hands. They have fought with evident or hidden weapons every effort toward social control. The tragedy of their whole situation is that they have never seen and do not seem to see now how the confusion they have brought upon us is the projection into regions of wealth, authority, and power of their own pitiful inner poverty.

We see, dramatically enough, what happens when a bank president maladministers his own kingdom of individual responsibility with no regard to ethical integrity. We do not see so clearly how each one of us through the conduct of his own life is making or unmaking our common world. We can at least begin with ourselves, rule, with a holy Christian order, our own little kingdoms though the world be anarchical, and maintain our own sanity though the world go mad. This is the first base line which Christian preaching can establish.

IV.

The second base line is righteousness—Christian righteousness. Those men whose administrations of their own lives have involved us in social calamity did not operate from that base line. They dismissed right and wrong as not within the sphere of practical politics, the policy of a state, or the conduct of finance. They never asked of any speculation, "Is this right?" or dismissed any project which promised to profit their inflated egotism because it was wrong. They pulled their houses down over their own heads because their souls had fallen in to begin with. The only pity is that they were not alone in the house.

The sad lack of any ethical standards in the whole jungle of predatory finance is an arresting fact upon which the *New York Times* lately took editorial space to comment. As figure

after figure came up for examination and left the stand branded
with intellectual shallowness and moral stupidity, the whole
ethic of their proud undertakings fell in like the dust of something long dead. They were left morally naked like Adam
and Eve in the garden and they did not know enough to hide
from God. Instead they went to Greece or back to Long Island.
They did not seem to know that there was a Tree of Good
and Evil in the garden of life. They only knew there was a
plum tree.

These men were, in a loose way, the ethical output of the
Christian church and they do it no credit. It must try again
and tell a morally disoriented age that immutable lines of right
and wrong run through every enterprise, every fellowship, every
deed, dream, desire, and that they are the first test and the
last judgment. That, as Farmer said in a noble sentence: "The
plumb-line which Isaiah saw against the wall of Jerusalem was
a segment of an infinite perpendicular let down from the stars."

The third Christian base line is concern for human well-
being. Thus stated it is a quite banal base line, an "of course"
base line. It should be bright with all the colors of the spectrum of human happiness. We have never entirely ignored
it. It is household law in all good homes, it is neighbor law
in all good neighborhoods. It is the finer part of all public
action.

The most critical would recognize the motivations of it as
the brighter strands in all our tangled web though, they would
maintain, it is always limited and too often defeated by the
machinery through which it has to work—including our own
human nature. They may be right, but what there is in
action of effective concern for human well-being is the salt
which has saved society from putrefaction.

The most assuring light along all our shadowed horizons
today is the growing recognition of it as the base line from

which industry and economics must be reoriented. We have been almost tragically misled by thing wealth, money wealth, security vault wealth, almost any kind of wealth save the well-being of all sorts and conditions of human folk. A society in which all children could sing themselves to sleep, as I hear sometimes, through his open window, the lovely little son of a neighbor singing himself to sleep, would be a better test of a civilization than all the wisdom of all the books. John Ruskin knew this also sixty years ago.*

"In fact, it may be discovered that the true veins of wealth are purple—and not in rock but in flesh—perhaps even that the final outcome and consummation of all wealth is in the producing as many as possible full-breathed, bright-eyed, and happy-hearted human creatures."† By such tests as these his England was, he said, strangely poor. But no one paid much attention to him then or since, being more interested in his unhappy love affairs and the tragedy of genius consumed in its own fires.

Jesus knew it eighteen centuries before Ruskin. It veins the Sermon on the Mount, it is the substance of His last reported parable. The tests which determined destiny were tests of humane attitude and action. His "right" and "left" were not the conservative and the radical, or the orthodox and the heretical. His "right" before the judgment seat of God were those who had served broken men according to the measure of their power. His "left" were those who had not heard the appeal of the Son of God behind the unhealed miseries

---

* No one could now render preachers a greater service than to give them a well-chosen anthology of Ruskin's writings in economics and allied subjects. It would be for them a source of wisdom and baptize their speech with a noble fire. Also they would be instructed in the art of preaching beyond the power of any teacher of homiletics to instruct them.

† *Unto This Last*, "The Veins of Wealth."

of life nor seen in the faces of the hungry, the marred visage of the suffering Servant. His church set up another judgment bar.

We have of late begun a little to see how the most telling condemnation of our prevailing economic system is its failure to accomplish its proper human ends. That is a purely economic condemnation. It would hold if ethical and religious tests were entirely ignored. Any system which fails in distributing economic wealth adequately to meet general human need is poor economics.

One does not preach to an engine which will not work or pray over it either—though the engineer may need the consolation and restraints of religion. There pragmatic test of it is, Will it run and carry its load? If not, it must be taken down and rebuilt. Our economic machinery pounds and does not carry its load. Our mistake has really been about the load. We are beginning to see it must be human well-being.

V.

The preacher can begin here. He has behind him the Hebrew prophets, the gospel of Jesus Christ, the experiences of twenty centuries, and the true genius of Christianity. Preaching down the front of human well-being will go far if it follows its line. It will carry with it vital principles of examination and judgment. It will demand and help to create a society in which general well-being is not as now a delusion of the privileged. It will have to define its own terms in terms of soul and station, society and state. It will not stop with material well-being. It will be concerned with well-being as wealth of character and inner resource.

It will be more concerned with a civilization of culture, to quote Principal Jacks, than a civilization of possession and power. It will insist upon wholeness of body, mind, and soul and restore to holiness its ancient, vital meanings. It will recall us to forgotten or undiscovered sources of well-being. Kipling has a lovely sentence about music which becomes soft and full of little sounds that chase each other on wings "across the broad, gentle flood of the main tune."

There can be no music of human well-being until, to use a figure I do not know how to use, there is a resolution into harmony of all the discordant elements in our social and economic systems, and the discordant elements in our own personalities. That music will be the basal orchestration of life. But so much of our happy well-being comes from the little things which chase one another on wings across the main current. What are they? What we have vision to see and ears to hear and grace to entertain.

Being fugitive and shy they cannot endure hate or hardness or too much haste. They are blue shadows across winter snow, the whisper of little flames upon a hearth, the smile of a child, the laughter of lovers, and the deep content of those who having lived long together need no words, but only being together. They are high clouds, the first wash of green across April pastures, or a broken furrow turned in steel blue March. They are music and the echo of a remembered poet's song, the hoarded wisdom of the wise, and the sun-given gold of a dream, half-dream, half-purpose.

"And all a wonder and a wild desire."

All such things as these, like Kipling's overtones of music, may accompany the main currents of well-being—if only they be secured—and without them all the finer music of life is mute.

Preaching can and must associate good-will with the quest

for well-being; this is its fourth base line. Good-will has a power to implement every endeavor as well as to orient it. Recent translations have made good-will the motif of the song which an unforgettable Christian legend believed the shepherds to have once heard above their starlit pastures. "Glory to God in heaven and on earth peace to men of good-will" lacks a little the cadence and majesty of the Gloria in Excelsis, but it is, after all, about what wise angels with long and trying experiences as guardians over us humans would sing.

They would know that the gift of peace to men of ill-will is futile and, though God may be abundantly ready to give it, it cannot be received save as good-will opens the door. With good-will as a base line, we may give an enabling power to Christian love which, for all our singing about it, praying for it, and professing to possess it, it does not seem hitherto to have had save in very limited regions and relations. Good-will is the ethical and volitional content of love, the root from which it grows.

Love is more than good-will; no need to say that. It has ardor, desire, imagination, romance in it. It clothes the beloved with grace and beauty. What it cares for seems

> "Appareled in celestial light,
>   The glory and the freshness of a dream."

It makes hard things easy, the second mile short, and upon the altars love builds no sacrifice is too costly to offer. The love of romantic attachment is apparently beyond our power either to summon or forbid. The regnancy of such love over command is the secret of its power—and its weakness. Christian love has an ethical province and is subject to our command. It is "glowing good-will," good-will with what St. Paul calls the "spiritual glow" in it. If a preacher for the articulation of his own mind should substitute these three words for "love" throughout his New Testament, his preaching would also gain in articulation.

He might even preach about good-will toward God and find it for himself and his congregation a key to open many doors and resolve many of the difficulties in which a clear, strong faith in God now finds itself. If one begins with no more than good-will toward whatever intimations of truth, beauty, and goodness he can discover in earth and sky and his fellow-men and himself, he may, if he follows those broken gleams high and far enough, reach the full light of the beatific vision.

Well, then, good-will is a base line. The three projections of it—Godward, manward, and inward—can orient the whole of life. It must have agencies through which to express itself, it needs much help from judgment and experience to determine what it should do when it has the power to be actually *good*-will. If it be good-will its judgment is always surer than the judgment of ill-will. Its decisions have the clarity of unselfishness. It is long-suffering and blessedly resourceful and nobly creative. There are few abysses in human relationship which cannot be bridged when good-will begins to build its spans from either side. There is no limit, apparently, to the havoc of ill-will.

The most mordant pages in Wells's *The Shape of Things to Come* are his "Note on Hate and Cruelty." His suggestion of a "hate map" of the world with its varying intensities of coloring after two thousand years of Christianity is like a nightmare, but it is not a dream. These hatreds, prejudices, passions hot from the pit are not abstractions, they live in the souls of living folks, are fed and fanned by human agents. How shall we ever get our souls and societies right till they are drained of hate and ill-will and sweetened, disinfected, and empowered by a good-will which washes in from the ocean of the love of God. This can be preached.

VI.

Fulness of life is another base line and the Christian goal
as well divinely validated. "I am come," said Jesus, "that they
might have life and have it above measure." Any road to
fulness of life is essentially a Christian road. The pity of life
—so many lives—is that so many quests go wrong because
we take the wrong roads. Life seems to defeat us by the
very simplicity of it. Because love and labor, friendship, the
happy use of mind, the holy use of sense, and the deepening
experiences of our lengthening years do not seem enough, we
adorn the lives we would love to live with the tapestry of
imagination.

We build, as George Eliot said, our castles in Spain without
taking account of what we ourselves are or should be to live
in them. We are eager for recognition and the sense and
acclaim of accomplishment when all the while the roads to
happiness and inner wealth are near and open. They are not
easy roads. No one has the right to say that. Perhaps we
miss the true fulness of life because it asks of us reconciliations
with our fortune and estates which we are not willing to
make, and so we beat ourselves out against our own limitations
or the estate to which it has pleased God to assign us.

There is another side to all this. The beauty and consolation of the beatitudes are recognized by all good Christians,
and little litanies are made of them in which, as they are read,
the congregation devoutly repeat: "Lord, be gracious unto us,
and help us to obtain this blessing." "Deliver us, Good Lord,
from any need of finding blessing in such ways as these" would
probably more correctly represent our dominant dispositions.
We think "divine discontent" a more telling topic than "I have
learned in whatsoever state I am to be content" and point to
the vigorous and aggressive Spirit of America with the bless-

ings thereupon attendant as an illustration of the direction in which the beatitudes ought really to be revised.

There is for all that a contentment which may become rich in fulness of life. Those virtues which the apostles of the will-to-power stigmatize as the morality of slaves have really been the true strength of civilizations which the will-to-power brought down in red ruin. We would better begin to study the art of the simple life; there is every indication we shall have to practice it. "I am instructed," said St. Paul, "in the art of life."

José Ortega y Gasset has two chapters in his remarkable book *The Revolt of the Masses* * which bear upon this whole matter with a penetrating insight. He is analyzing the forces which have come into action with the nineteenth and twentieth centuries, but his insights bear upon life as a whole and the tensions of our human estate. We live, he says, at a time which believes itself "fabulously capable of creation" but does not know what to create. Its unbelievable knowledge and technical skill defeat themselves because they have no sure sense of end. Life, escaping the grasp of its inherited controls, has become completely unsubmissive. This is due, Señor Ortega believes, to the "dizzy increase" of population and mechanical device in the last one hundred years. "Heaps of human beings" have been dumped on the historic scene too fast to "saturate them with traditional culture." One has the impression of a primitive man suddenly risen in the midst of a very old civilization. This neo-primitive has, he thinks, a healthier, stronger soul than the sons of the past, but he does not yet know what to do with it.

Civilization waits upon the brink of disaster for the emergence of a new discipline. But discipline takes time and the

* W. W. Norton & Co., Inc., New York, 1932.

situation is so desperately urgent.   All this is true enough, far more true than the conclusions of Spengler and his school, who gather with their premature post-mortems around the bed of dying Western civilization and will not leave the curtains decorously drawn or allow the sick order to die in peace.   Forms and orders may disappear in tumult and tragedy.   But Western humanity was never more alive.

Ortega's insights need little restatement to go far beyond the present crisis.   They bear upon the profound paradox of human life.   Man's soul, his sense of "otherness" from his world, his limitless urge to be and to do beyond his seeming power, his homesickness for an order beyond his own, are his doom and his glory.   He carries the burden of wings which will not let him be at home on earth and sustain him precariously as he seeks to leave it.   There was, the biologist tells us, a stage in evolution when this was true of all winged life. It took a long time to make a bird and what failed in the adventure of flight either became a fossil or remained a reptile.

We have of late sought either the wrong use for our wings or else have refused to use the wings we really have.   We have been strangely slow to appreciate the possible wealth of happy contentment which might attend a manner of life to which the whole material side of life made only relatively simple contributions.   We have instead followed the fascinating and apparently limitless air-ways opened for us by our power to invent and create.   There our possibilities seemed boundless, there we surrendered our imaginations, there we lost our sense of proportion, and there the possible debacle of cilivization has opened before us.

VII.

It seems almost unforgivably naïve to offer no more than the Christian evangel of a cross-given fulness of life to a world crowded with men and women who have not even the barest necessities of life for whom death behind a barricade seems preferable to life without resource or hope. But it is not impossible and it is not naïve to preach fulness of life to civilizations which have forgotten that neither the state nor anything in it has any excuse for being save as they secure fulness of life for all God's children.

The President of the United States has of late taken that very phrase to name the ends he is urging the republic to seek. He may use it loosely and with his own perplexities as to the roads which will lead to it. That he uses it at all is a blessed sign of the emergence of new visions and new values. It is only a base line—granted—but once facing out from it a region opens across which there is a noble calling of trumpets.

The goal upon which so many lines of inquiry and social experiment are now beginning to converge is the discovery of an adequate control for our overpowered and underhumanized civilizations. Systems so irreconcilably opposed as fascism and political liberalism may be in complete opposition as to method; the end sought is the same: adequate social control. I do not think control the right word, at least so far as it carries only a suggestion of restraint. Life needs control only as a river needs banks and a free way to the sea. We need not less but more *élan vital;* not this or that dam but noble and open and rightly directed channels through which the great currents of life may flow.

We do not need a *frein vital*—the pull of a bridle rein upon the bit of life—nearly so much as a *règlement souverain*—a supreme ordering of life through an articulation of impulse, action, and control into a fulness of being and action whose liberty is noble obedience, whose obedience is perfect liberty. This is the office of Christianity if Christianity has any office at all. Its divine purpose is not restraint but liberty. "Ye shall know the truth and the truth shall set you free."

Liberty under an inward and spiritual discipline lies at the very heart of St. Paul's conception of Christian faith and the Christian life. The Christian base lines of life do control but only as the compass and the chart control a richly freighted liner as she seeks her desired haven. The only sure control is the direction of all the force and promise of life toward fulness of life.

I do not see for the life of me how else we can reach a disoriented age than from these base lines. It is all so simple and so complex, so difficult and so easy, so possibly near and so perilously remote. I should think our great danger now is that the masters of our militant states will not let their people alone till civilization can reorient itself. They are deluded with grandiose policies, half-mad with a nationalism which has forgotten what the state is for. They see so far ahead that they cannot see the bleeding humanity out of whose bodies and souls they build their roads toward murky destiny.

"Earth is sick and heaven is weary
Of the hollow words that states and kingdoms utter
When they talk of truth and justice."

The church can at least, and if need be, take up, as its own cross, the cause of humanity broken upon the crosses they are making. It has had a long dealing with a cross upon which pride and power broke a Man's body and a woman's heart and by which they themselves were finally broken.

VIII.

No one name is entirely right for what we have been considering. I have called them base lines. They are perhaps more accurately the creative Christian attitudes; or else they are the Christian approaches. If they are "approaches" they have behind them the divine authority of the Christian ethic, the Christian creeds, and, as far as it can be enforced, the Christian church. The strength of Christianity is in its power to approach a world of dissolving standards, a world whose faith is undone, whose hopes are deeply shadowed, and whose experiments bring it little assurance of their success and many omens of tragic failure, with something which has itself outlasted civilizations, in which all the truly victorious experiences of the West are funded, and which claims its own authority from a source above the stormy fluctuations of any human order, its wisdom from the mind of the Eternal.

I think, however, that preaching will do most for the modern mind and mood which begins just where they are and carries them on along such lines as we have just been considering. There will always be a wealth of definite material, a general advance along this front will sooner or later include every situation and every relationship. The men and women behind the gray walls of Auburn State Prison, the broken and lonely who ask now no more than bread, the "first enemy of society" and the great friends of society, the fellowship of our own about our own hearthstones and the alien on the far shores of the seven seas are all within the scope of it.

Nor will the preacher be able to stop till he has reached again the heights of Christian faith. The great approaches— good-will, human well-being, ethical integrity, fulness of life, the redemption of our stained and broken human estate—all open out and up. Each step to bring them near or make them true involves something more. They disclose their own unescapable relationships with and their equally unescapable dependence upon further ranges of reality.

They involve brave adventures of faith, they disclose even in the quest for them the unseen and enduring foundations of all faith. They discover in their progress the redemptive significance of the cross of Jesus Christ. They summon resources, they begin to play a music upon instruments of whose existence we had not dreamed because we had not before heard the music. They begin to demand a reach of time enough for which time is not enough. We begin like the mariners with whom St. Paul took ship, we begin in the dark and the storm to suspect that there is land ahead.

There is no nodding parishioner inside any church lost in his own reveries and the discreet shadows of the sanctuary who has not somewhere a spot with which a vital contact can be made, some questing outreach of his spirit through which he may be approached in such preaching. There are spiders, Fabre says, which when their brief sunlit day is come climb out of earth darkness by what is nearest to them—low though it be—and spin their lines of silver web, gossamer frail, abroad to the winds. Along whatever thread catches and holds they set out upon whatever adventure an arachnid is destined to. They have made themselves a bridge and trusted its cables to the universe.

Of an October day all the low grasses, the fugitive growths of the fields are shining with these silver lines but you have to stoop to see them. Every assembled congregation is throwing out filaments like that, hopes and fears and needs and questings, seeking for something to fasten on. Preaching is, among so many other things, the power to see them—one must stoop sometimes—and follow them back to their sources in the hearts of men. They may seem frail but they are ways to reach a soul. They are much the same for all sorts and conditions of people at any one time, nor do they, I think, change their character across lands and epochs as much as we think. Men and women are always asking for what they cannot live without. They are seeking footholds on slippery slopes, understanding of situations they cannot reconcile.

The answers must in a way be the old answers. They can, to repeat—and this needs much repeating—be given in a way to suit them to the contemporaneous mind and situation. They get their orientation from the funded Christian wisdom-about-life, from the Way, the Truth, and the Life of Jesus Christ. They get their content from here-and-now. Unless they bear directly upon here-and-now situations, they are no more than a web of words spun, this time, by the preachers and making no contact with what is before him.

Whatever telling preaching is being done in the American pulpit at present begins with these base lines of Christian faith, purpose, values, ends, and methods. It is sensitive to definite forms of need, desire, and thought. It is vividly aware of its world, it has a power like the poet's power to invest simple things with timeless meaning and beauty. It has imagination and honest passion, and the power of it is in the truth of it. It can never lack occasion or material and it carries Christward and crossward. Such preaching does not live by the day; it is an accent of the enduring wisdom of the Master of the churches.

CHAPTER IX

THE GEOGRAPHY OF A SERMON

IN OUR consideration of what must always be for a preacher the fascinating subject of preaching, we have used more than one analogy; that preaching is like a tree whose vitality depends upon its root-hold in life and experience; that, like a surveyor's map or a navigator's chart, it must be oriented to the sovereign base lines of Christian faith and attitudes. There is another analogy which applies to any single sermon and I do not know any other which suits so well the purpose of this chapter.

It would be possible to make a map of sermon-land, a curious map, whose best analogy in terrestrial geography would be the drainage basin of a river system. For any sermon is a point at which many tributaries meet and some unescapable necessity should direct its course as rivers have their channels made for them. The terrain of it is the minds and spirits of men and all the constitution of our human fellowship. Its tablelands touch the infinite mystery of life. Its backgrounds are the exalted and sometimes cloud-possessed regions of Christian faith and doctrines. It includes the heights and depths of experience, pleasant valleys, sunlit slopes, and whatever else, if one use the conceit of a map, might be added. Its geography is the geography of the soul. Who can make a map of that?

If one should think of the hinterlands and horizons of a

sermon, that too would fit into the analogy of the map—
a map which has suddenly become a great landscape. Hinterlands are the regions where rivers have their sources and
from which streams of trade flow down to fill a harbor with
ships. Horizons are bounds, but what bounds! They belong more to imagination than any map, they must be wide
and far enough for the unfulfilled and the unpossessed. The
amplitude of life, like the amplitude of a land, is in the heights
from which it issues and the seas toward which it flows.
These invest it with wealth and wonder. So with preaching.
It is not quite Carlyle's "a little gleam between two eternities"; it is a point upon which great tributaries converge,
from which great issues might flow out.

I spent an hour last night in a minister's study, a plain
room furnished with a desk, a chair or so, and book-lined
walls. Some of the books were likely more worn by much
moving than by much reading and of a sad, inner dustiness,
though once the dust may have been pregnant. He was much
interested in prayer—perhaps because it was Lent—and showed
me books thereupon painfully written, though everything that
prayer can be was said four thousand years ago on a Chaldean
tablet:

"O my queen, daughter of the shining heaven,

. . . . . .

The worshiper on whom thou lookest is rich in power,
. . . his life is prolonged.
I have no mother—thou art my mother;
I have no father—thou art my father,

. . . . . .

Thou hast given me the breath of life,
. . . in thy shadow I will reverently dwell."

His books were only windows, clear or clouded, through

which there shone some gleam of insight, some report or other upon our timeless quest. He will go of a Sunday to such a pulpit as a minor denomination in Auburn supplies and share with a congregation of limited estate the grace of his kind and devout spirit, his ripened wisdom-about-life, and his faith. His prayers will owe little to any book but they will lift those for whom he prays above the narrow bounds of their own lives to rest beneath the shadow of the Eternal.

His hinterlands are not in his worn study. They reach back through all his knowledge and training and personality to his sustaining confidence. His horizons do not end at the back pews of his church; they reach out to the ultimate issues of life. The veritable walls of his study were too vast to be discerned through any winter twilight.

Every sermon, I am trying to say, has behind it a widening succession of always ascending sources; it must be directed toward widening ranges of duty, character, and wealth of life. One could almost as in a map name its bench levels. They would start from a preacher's manuscript or notes and go back and up through the whole content of his mind and his power to use it, his training, his theology, his understanding of the ways and meanings and needs of life. Preaching gets its substance and power from its spiritual and intellectual watersheds. If it be not fed from great sources it will become a dry river bed of pebbly words worn smooth by long usage. If it take no free course toward the enduring ends of life it will be like the rivers which lie as threads across the map of Persia ending nowhere save in little salt lakes, like the "lost rivers" of our own arid West.

I.

What, then, are the hinterlands of creative preaching? I should put above and behind them all, taking a noble phrase from John Fiske, "the everlasting reality of religion." We have taken account of the critics who maintain that preaching is by no means the only way of keeping the sense of the reality of religion alive, and never the best way. They have a case. Worship, the ministry of the altar, and the absolution of the priest were the native forms of religion. But it is difficult to see how sacramental and liturgical religion can endure unless preaching furnish it interpretation and support. Preaching cannot do this unless it be itself veined with the reality of religion and not alone veined with it but finding there its vital breath.

How preaching can persuade the modern mind of "the everlasting reality of religion" no one can say without making a book of it also and he will not say it then. He will only write a book, if he knows enough, about the books which are just now exploring the reality of religion from every possible approach. A very great deal which is being done in these regions especially in the relation of science to religion needs much "stepping down" before it can possibly be preached. Even then it will be done at the preacher's own risk.

There are less than a half-dozen living scientists able so to simplify the conclusions reached, through the aid of unbelievably difficult mathematics,* about the nature of the physical universe as to make them partially intelligible to most of us, or suggest their bearings upon religious faith. Bishop Barnes seems to be the only English-speaking clergyman who can meet them upon their own grounds.

A wise preacher will for the present leave all this to the specialist. Reading "Scientific Theory and Religion" is a better discipline in intellectual humility than a preparation

---

* Modern science seems to be approaching Pythagoras's supposition (according to Bacon), "Numbers to be the principles and original of things," only they substitute formulæ for numbers.

for next Sunday's sermon. "The Fitzgerald-Lorenz Contraction" may prove the length of a rod moving with the velocity of light to be zero but it has little bearing upon our very human needs and burdens. The unpredictable action of the more hypothetical constituents of an atom may prove that we are free moral agents. It is at the best, however, a highly hazardous proof, being entirely at the mercy of the next theory about the atom, and it will leave the man cold who is struggling with the perplexing alternatives of daily life. What are protons, electrons, or neutrons to him or he to them? One may find permission to believe in God because Riemannian space, though unbounded, is still finite but the weary and heavy laden will get no help from a God whose throne is beyond the time-space continuum. They want a God "who is a very present help in time of trouble."

These regions are as remote from the needs and experiences of life as belted Orion from the shadowed room in which this is being written. (A fire on one's own hearthstone of a winter night means more than Orion and the Pleiades.) All this must immediately be qualified. Rigel and the fire on a hearthstone are kindred flames; to find if we can what the source is from which both are kindled is the noblest compulsion of our minds. Religion is vitally associated with the conclusions of science and philosophy. They are all contributions to our understanding of ourselves and our universe, and there must be some harmony between them if we are not to be put to permanent intellectual confusions. They are interpretations of what George A. Gordon called the infinite mystery for which it is our doom and our glory to seek some solution.

Widening knowledge has in no wise diminished it but only brought it more near and magnified the empire of it. The very table upon which one writes now pulses with mystery, and every common sight, common no longer, is "appareled in celestial light." This has not banished religion; it has supplied it provinces for a new empire, nebulæ for new worlds. But religion must organize its empire and create its own world of reality after its own nature. It carries on from where science stops. Religion is an interpretation of the infinite mystery. It is still more the way in which we who love and suffer, seek and hope, direct our lives and carry through our great adventure.

II.

There is just now a habit of calling religion only "wishful thinking," our pathetic effort to build for ourselves a shelter in cosmic loneliness.* As though on a winter night one should build a fire on his own hearthstone, draw his curtains and forget the north wind and the outer darkness—though they are still there. The friends of religion may, I think, accept that definition without apology, if only they carry it far enough. Wishful thinking is nothing to be ashamed of if only the wish be nobly creative. It is the secret of whatever power we possess, of whatever growth we have reached.

There should be a better word than "wish," which has an unfortunate association with poets and tellers of fairy tales. It may be a detached-from-reality word, a sibilant escape-from-what-we-are word. We use it for conventional exchanges of courtesy and New Year's greetings and do no more about it. But that is not of the whole of wishing. It is always some projection of desire which may become a purpose, a program, a deed. What we do and what we become are in some fashion the issue of what we wish, especially in those regions where we have freedom of choice and action. Wishful thinking is

---

* Or, to use a noble phrase of Bacon's, though he used it of poetry and not religion, to give "some shadow of satisfaction to the mind of man in those points where the nature of things doth deny it."

an aspect of our power to build out of many alternatives a world shaped to our need and vision. It is an expression of what is the supreme distinction of human nature—the creative spirit, and who shall say out of what unplumbed depths that comes.

"The most important fact," says Tagore,* "that has come into prominence along with the change of direction in our evolution is the possession of a spirit . . . with a surplus far in excess of the requirements of the biological animal in man." Out of this surplus, this margin of freedom to dream and think and act and ask and be, man has made his human world with all the splendor and the pity, the sanctity and the sin of it. "Righteousness, truth, great endeavors, empire, religion, enterprise, heroism, and prosperity, the past and the future dwell in the surpassing strength of the surplus." Thus we build and shall always build. Industry builds out of earth-stuff fitted to its purpose industrial orders which feed and shelter and, a little, enrich us. Art and literature build out of our surplus of creative vision an order of beauty, music, noble speech, and moving song. And religion?

It also is a creative adventure. It builds out of the infinite mystery its own world of faith, experience, and understanding. It is at once the expression of our need, the revelation of our insight, and the final source of all our at-homeness in a world to which we are both native and strangely alien.

All our worlds are like that; we make them out of what is furnished us. The scientist's universe of four dimensions in which flying yardsticks shrink to nothing and space ends with no space beyond it † is made by mathematics. Since

---

* *The Religion of Man*, The Macmillan Company, New York, 1931, a book of marvelous insight. Chaps. II and III. By permission of The Macmillan Company.

† A totally unscientific statement. Barnes calls it "a prejudice of the imagination" but admits that the paradox occasionally puzzles a mathematician.

no one ever came to the end of space or saw a yardstick going 186,000 miles a second, there is no proof of its existence save the integrity and consistency of the mathematical process checked off by what experimentation is possible. The mathematician believes it a real universe because he trusts his processes. They may carry him beyond experiment but they bring him nearer ultimate reality.

We do not make our human experimental world of space and time out of mathematical formulæ. We make it out of sight and sound, movement and touch. There may be, as Eddington suggests, any amount of universe building material in stock out of which, if we were different builders with other tools, we might build an engrossing variety of worlds strangely different from the one we know. (If we had, for example, seven senses instead of six!)* But, being what and how we are, we make our own out of sounds we can hear and colors we can see and wood which, in spite of the dance of its atoms, is assuringly strong, and out of what else makes it dear and steadfast and *real*.

I would underscore "real." The reality of any world we live in is its coherence, constancy; what it gives us to work with which does work, and its contribution to the integrity of our lives. We have no choice about the lower stories of our world of reality. We work wood in terms of grain and texture and not in terms of protons and neutrons. These necessities seem to be forced upon us by the conjoined action of our own faculties and what we use them on.

I have long believed that our ways of thinking, seeing, and all the rest have been shaped for us by an unbelievably long association of once plastic forms of life with what life has to live with and live on. We take the form of the mold into which we have been cast, even in our minds; we call the

---

* We probably have. I have included "temperature sense" in the six.

This fellow's psychology must be very musty!

world reasonable because our reason was developed according to its ways—we are microcosm of its macrocosm. I am not philosopher enough to say so convincingly—though it has been said.

There seem, however, to be upper stories in the house of life and the vaster house of the infinite mystery where we have some choice about what we shall build and what material we shall use. We can build a good human world or a bad human world. We have never yet built either entirely and finally but our long experimentation seems to prove that we have both choice and power in the matter. We do seem to have some choice between sense and self-restraint, between good-will and ill-will, between helping others and using them; between living for greedy getting—like a good many very high executives—and living for noble being—like very unconsidered men and women who never had a bonus in their bare, patient, laborious lives. They only paid for the high executives' bonuses.

This world of moral character and relationship about which we have some alternatives of choice, for the building of which there is a proper building material, is also a *real* world. Its tests of reality are the coherence of it, the well-being which it secures, the fact that we can work together in building it and that it shelters and satisfies what seems (I am using "seem" so often—to beg no disputed questions) most human and best in promise in our little lives.

We seem to grow like it in building it, as if its beams and girders were actually in our own souls. "That," said one of the noblest Upanishads, "That art *thou*." We have some persuasion, which grows as we build, that its foundations have been laid for us by another Builder and that, though it seems to be plastic to our touch, the moral order has its own architectonic laws which are themselves of the nature of things, so that all things work for and with us when we build at their bidding and against us when we challenge or disobey them.

As we venture further out on the verge of the infinite mystery—or as we ascend the stairs of life which wind upward through it—we seem to have another and more awesome freedom, the freedom to build our houses of faith. We must always extend the frontiers of all our tested knowledge into some vaster region to find the sense and meaning of what we think we know. Experience is always demanding more experience to complete it. We cannot go far down any road until we have come to faith-land. The scientist has one name for it, the philosopher another. The agnostic may refuse to name it. The devout call it religion, the saint calls it "the practice of the presence of God." By all the tests of reality which apply to any other world we live in, the world of religion is real. But we must live in it to know that.

Religion has its own country and we cannot really know it unless we live in it. Preaching can at least trace its frontiers and indicate its wealth and ask the doubting at least to explore it. The reality of religion begins for us in the reality of our teachableness, in our love of goodness, in the upreach of our spirits. It increases with our growing sensitiveness to any intimation of the enduring. It is perfected in our power to see through any goodness the gleam of a master goodness and trace through light and shadow the pattern which Eternal Kindness has conceived. Then we learn to say, though the lesson is not always easy, that "the heart of the Eternal is most wonderfully kind."

Prayer and praise will be the natural voices of those who thus become citizens of the spiritual order. They will see along the horizons of the lengthening years a light from beyond the hills of time. It is too much to expect a faith thus evoked, the reality of religion thus intimately known, to be the same for all sorts and conditions of people, but something must be left to the mercy of God. His understanding, one may dare believe, goes out to meet any who seek Him before they themselves know that He has met them.

III.

This is only the first far hinterland of preaching. If it be Christian it will mediate the reality of religion through the Way, the Truth, and the Life of Jesus Christ. Such approaches to the whole field of religious experience as have so far been considered are not definite enough for the preacher or glowing enough for the congregation. I do think they suggest a method, if one may use so cold a word, of helping perplexed folk to think out and live through their perplexities. They represent the general approach of very thoughtful leaders who seek to maintain the integrity of religion against the scientific and humanistic drive. They can, as Wieman and others have shown, be brought down from cold and foggy heights to furnish a support for a warm, religious devotion.*

It seems, however, a needless task to build such approaches to religious reality when there is already a sure and sunlit way. Christianity is that way—essentially; as Jesus knew it; lived it; died in the redemptive creation of it. There is the true religious hinterland of Christian preaching. There are its message sources, there its high command. Whatever is cold and

---

* There is a clear road from Wieman's *The Wrestle of Religion with Truth* to his *Methods of Private Religious Living,* and it is not fair to dismiss the first as too rare a field for any but trained mountain climbers with an oxygen tank in reserve without seeing what can actually come of it all as he comes down to our own hearthstones in the second. *The Wrestle of Religion with Truth* was meant for the campus of the University of Chicago and other similar intellectual tablelands. *Methods of Private Religious Living* is meant for "seekers" who want to be religious and do not know how.

distant in the "wrestle of religion with truth" becomes near and ardent in the Christian wrestle with life. The Christian methods of religious living were incarnate in One for whom the Unseen blossomed from Galilean fields, for whom the mountain slopes were sanctuaries, who spoke to His Father from the bitter agony of His cross as a man speaks to a friend. He left His followers a way of life which He believed would bring them a similar assurance.

"The Way" is the oldest name for Christianity; it supplies still its timeless power. That way empowers and enfranchises. It is the lovelit, divinely guided way to integrity of soul and fruitful goodnesses. It might be the way to world peace, to the solution of our militant economic confusion. Its signboards will guide us to the fulness of life which the Master said He came to bestow. Those who follow that Kings Highway will find themselves in "God's country."

Religion is vulnerable to intellectual attack and vitally dependent upon rational defense. Even religious thinkers like Newman who carried on a war without a truce with rationalism have had to rationalize their own position. A religion without a foundation which seems reasonable to its followers has taken a mortal wound. But people do not generally reason themselves into religion or out of it either. It is a way of life whose reality depends upon their own responses and obediences. There are ways of living, hospitalities of the spirit in which realities seem quite sure which in another temper seem remotely unreal. Sometimes love and goodness become for the best of men and women only dreams in a bitter world. Sometimes they are more sure than the sun in the sky because we have moved into another spiritual climate. Even the saints and the psalmists have lived under changing skies of spiritual certainty.

It is not the task of the preacher to argue the reality of religion from the pulpit.* He has no right to be there unless in some regnant aspect of it it is real to him. His task is to get people to live where religion is. They are more likely to fail in that through their ignorance of the Way than the perverseness of their wills. They must be helped toward the kind of life to which religion is native and where the sureness of it steals upon their spirits almost unawares. Others are already living in some province of religion and do not know it. There is a marvelous insight in the New Testament of which preaching does not make enough; ". . . they that abide in love abide in God." All who live in good-will, in the quest for goodness, are already in God's country. They need only to have their vision a little more cleared to say, "Surely the Lord is in this place and I know it not." This is the noblest task of preaching.

If it be urged that all this stops short of the entire Christian gospel the writer admits it. Everything cannot be said in one book. He has written, mostly, with certain phases of the mind of the time in view. But our inherited types of preaching are not so rich in results as any friend of the church could wish. If there is any way at all to widen their appeal and make preaching more creatively telling, there should be a place for it. It is our conjoint task. Nothing has been said here which forbids any kind of preaching which might reach and help and save a world which needs so much saving.

---

* Or the existence of God. I doubt whether argument ever does religion much good or whether "conversations about God" do much more than brighten a conference of inquiring youth or supply the resourceful editor of a religious journal exceedingly good material. Certainly the books which once proved the existence of God are gathering dust. One may gravely wonder whether their modern equivalents will not suffer the same fate (most books do). "No one," said Deist Collins, "doubted the existence of Deity until the Boyle lectures undertook to prove it." The philosopher must ignore this epigram in his study and the teacher in the classroom. But the preacher should never forget it in the pulpit.

Even so with all the "apologetics" I have read.

Moreover, the very lines which are here suggested will converge, as they are followed through, upon the Christian doctrines. The great creeds have a timeless authority. They are rooted in what George Eliot, in a noble phrase, called "the massive and ardent spiritual experience of humanity." The stained and broken estate of human nature, its immemorial cry for salvation, the divine participation in the travail of our souls of which the cross is the symbol, our need to be reached and changed beyond our power to change ourselves are all stations of the Christian Way. No preaching can follow that road with power and fidelity which does not follow their direction.

IV.

But they do need interpretation. "Orthodox" preaching will take no harm from doing that; it will gain in power by doing it. To interpret is not to doubt but to strengthen and illumine. It furnishes the inarticulate a voice and translates symbols into a living language. The scientist is an interpreter beneath whose touch dust and stars take on another meaning. The philosopher is an interpreter whose systems seek a reconciling unity of our inner and outer worlds. The poet is an interpreter for whom the yellow records of an old Roman murder trial become the many-faceted play of hate and greed and stainless purity and the power of love to save through nothing more than being love.

The artist is an interpreter, finding in the face of one old woman all the pathos of all the years. The musician sets to the music of an unfinished symphony thoughts that lie too deep for tears. Religion is interpretation. The story of its long procession can be told as interpretation and told truly. Theology itself was interpretation to begin with, written out of life. The doctrines of St. Paul were first of all, in his "divided self," his surrender in the Damascene desert, in his death with Christ to all his past. The rigidities of Augustine the theologian are molten in the *Confessions of Augustine the Saint*. And so on always.

The great theologies can be put back into life again: all of them. But it takes the interpreter to do it. Sin needs interpretation: being "lost" needs interpretation—there are so many ways of being lost and so many lost folk. Salvation needs interpretation, the cross needs interpretation. It is planted deep in life; every flower by the wayside which lives a summer out and dies with the seeds of another summer's growth at the heart of it is not alien to it. Whenever love bears and shares and suffers to save the beloved the cross is there. Vicarious atonement is not a form of words, it is the law which binds us into one bundle and the power by which love and goodness lift the broken out of their pitiful dust.

Above all, the experiences of life need interpretation. The more paralyzing doubts of most folk are not philosphical or scientific. They grow out of the difficulty of reconciling pain and loss and sorrow and defeat with the love of an all-wise and all-powerful God. Job wrestled with that on his dust heap and all Job's kin have been wrestling with it ever since.

Preaching may wisely address itself to all these aspects of life and find therein a vital field. They cannot be disposed of by calling the problems of evil and suffering insoluble. They must be interpreted and the preaching which interprets them, if it do not take its departure from the cross, will come to the healing shadow of it before its interpretation is done. For how shall there be justice and love at the heart of the moral order if justice and love do not share all the travail of life, go down themselves into life's darkest depths and climb with it every Golgotha? This may be the meaning of the creedal article we omit: "He descended into Hell."

V.

Preaching is fed, of course, from the books especially intended for the vocation. Any preacher can find so much good advice about his reading as to make any exploration of this particular hinterland unnecessary here. Books of ruling ideas, pregnant books are worth more to the preacher than sapless books of great weight. "No preacher," a wise friend once said, "should read a book he could write himself"—meaning, I suppose, that one gets little help from books with whose general range of ideas he is himself familiar. He would better read twice an outstanding book in each department than pile around him too many of them.

Literature and art, poetry and the drama certainly belong to the hinterland of any noble preaching. They themselves are interpreters of life. They kindle the imagination—a precious faculty for any preacher. They contribute the magic of style, they bring color and light, and they say with wings what wise books often say with lead, and say it therefore all the more wisely. Something of their distinction will touch a sermon with a gleam and glory which reveal the preacher's comradeship with those elect spirits who, toiling tirelessly for excellence, share their possession of it with all their fellow-seekers.

Any preacher's preaching has behind it his training, the whole of it: heredity, home, and all his schools. Recent study of American churches and their ministry indicates far too many preachers who do not seem to have gone to school enough, but preaching itself is not the creation of the schools. They may do much in critical training but the faculty for it is essentially an endowment of the individual.

It does not always come to the theological schools with very capable students. In conspicuous cases it has never gone to the seminary at all (Lyman Abbott for example). There is no absolute constant between the force of the church's ministry and its percentage of scholastically trained men.* In addition capable ministers are really self-trained. In the end they make or unmake themselves. This hinterland of training is then quite uneven but it is there in some form.

Nearer still to every sermon is the preacher's life experience. Modernistic psychologists of an irreverent turn suggest that most preachers are really preaching to themselves. They say that with a proper insight one can see through the sermon into the preacher's soul. Preaching need not be ashamed of that unless the inner life out of which it comes be itself shameful. If there be between the preacher and the congregation an identity of experience and aspiration, then in preaching honestly to himself he is preaching effectively to them. I do not know what other sources, shot through with immediate power and passion, the preacher can draw on comparable with the drama of his own soul. It will all depend upon the range and veracity of his own experience and the extent to which it is humanly representative. It will depend also upon how he uses it.

If he use it jaggedly to give a point to dulness, it may be an impertinence. If he use it over-emotionally, it will only start a fire of shavings. If he use it to fill the gaps in which he has really nothing to say, it will be a broken reed to lean on. If he have no other message than the story of his "experience" he will move often. But if what he says is rooted

---

* That statement is open to question.

in his own victories or defeats; if he bring to the sorrowing the comfort wherewith he himself has been comforted, to the sick in spirit the medicine by which he himself has been healed, and to those much at sea the harbors in which he has found peace, such preaching will have a noble power.* Where else can preaching find the hiding place of power?

VI.

Since such things as these are, in descending order, tributary to any sermon, it is possible to speak of the geography of a sermon and to use the analogy of the drainage basin of a river to some useful purpose. We try sometimes in our classroom work to draw this map in loose, chalky outlines. There is not room enough for it on any blackboard but one may indicate a series of half circles one within the other and we name them very much in the order they have been named here: the reality of religion; the Christian mediation of religion; the preacher's backgrounds and experience, and the like. Across it all from top to bottom we draw a swelling "V." Next Sunday's sermon, we say, should be where the lines meet. Everything included between them and the unbounded region back to which they open combine to make just that one sermon.†

Now what is just behind the apex is extraordinarily important since it controls the choice of text and topic and specific organization of content. Here the lines should become very definite; they must focus upon something, upon a need, a purpose, or a situation; there they must focus, and on

---

* Arthur John Gossip has done this with great power. See, for example, "But When Life Tumbles In, What Then?"—*The Hero in Thy Soul*, Charles Scribner's Sons, New York, 1929.

† If the reader, most likely to be a preacher, cares to make such a map he will see what I mean.
It will be like this: He may name the lines as he pleases.

NOTE. SEE BACK INSIDE PAGE FOR AN ENLARGED ILLUSTRATION FROM THE PAPER JACKET OF THIS BOOK.—

something worth the concentration. Dr. Harry Emerson Fos-
dick does not, he says, begin with a subject; he begins with
an object. His sermons are meant to do something for the
very human needs and situations he discovers along all the
fronts of his rich human contacts.

His preaching drains from august heights of faith and understanding. It is fed by all his wisdom and culture and
the wealth of his own mind and spirit. It is music, passion,
power, and art in three thousand words. But the telling thrust
of it is the drive of his spear-point upon those realities of
our human estate here and now for which Christianity has
a message and saving power. Because he knows his time
he may trust to the viewless waves of the radio a message
which is pertinent from sea to sea. Because he knows what
is in the hearts of men he speaks to every listener as though
they two were alone.   All preaching should be like that.

Out of what reaches back and up from his study, reaching also down and out through him, the preacher chooses
what should be said on any Sunday to those *there*. He will
not always be able to explain his choice. It will be controlled
by his reasoned sense of what his people need, by some insistent pressure in his own mind and spirit, by a gleam of
insight through the dark. If he preach only because Sunday
is coming, he will choose at random and doubt his call when
he is done. If what he says *must* be said because first of all
it has possessed him and will give him no peace till he has
said it, he will discover for himself and his congregation the
secret of the Pentecostal wind and flame.

The controls consciously used or unconsciously obeyed will
change from Sunday to Sunday. They will reflect a shared
sorrow or some signal happiness, inconstant days and constant
seasons. They will reflect the blessed continuities of life and
labor and love. They will deal with the unusual and the

challenging. They will take their departure from white winter silences, from the vernal rapture of a world reborn, from
the happy gold of ripened harvest fields, and the tapestry
of autumnal forests.

They will follow the contours of the Christian year and
furnish a voice for its fasts and festivals. They will be wise
to do that, for all the drama of Christian redemption is thus
set in the frame of time, and something immemorial, older
than the Christian drama and native to the pilgrimage of
the soul through time and a changing world, is set in that same
frame.

The institutional needs of his church with its background
of denominational enterprises and programs will direct preaching whether the preacher like it or not. Preaching does not
really stoop from its high estate when it underwrites a budget
or keeps a church itself alive and growing. It may protest
—and justly—against being judged by statistics of attendance
and offerings as though Pegasus were harnessed to a cart but
that, among other things, is what it is for. If Pegasus has
wings he should occasionally use them to lift earthy enterprises
into his own native air.

These are in part what unite to make a single sermon. One
may press and turn the suggestion of the map as he pleases
and add what more is needed. He will, if he brood over
it, remember how rivers take their color from the regions which
they drain and so are clear or earth-stained. He will remember also that they have their singing rapids and their silent pools.
He will know how sometimes his little stream runs bank-full and
how again it shrinks to a thread. If he care more for psychology than geography he will say that our blackboard map
is a poor thing—and I will not quarrel with him.

What we are actually dealing with is, he can insist, far
more imponderable. He will conceive a sermon in terms of

association lines and suggestion and find such a telephone switchboard as we saw at Chicago last summer a better analogy than any map. Upon that switchboard we saw a red light take its appointed road through a thousand possible contacts till it found the line-end for which it was meant and there it went out, because connection was made and the message could go through. Preaching is making message connection.

No matter what figure one uses it takes life and vision, truth and faith, need and answer, the divine and the human to make any sermon. It is poor enough at its best, foolish enough at its wisest, sputtering with static as its clearest, but if it establish one brief contact between us and the Unseen and Eternal it has served its ends.

VII.

And what are its ends? Such a map as has been suggested is only half drawn. It may roughly indicate the sources and controls, near and far, of preaching. It does not indicate the horizons, near or far, out toward which it moves. No map can ever do that, only a single singing poet's line a little changed: "From the great deep to the great deep it goes"—

"From that great deep, before our world begins,

. . . . . .

From that true world within our world we see,
Whereof our world is but the bounding shore."

And out again through life and faith to their enduring issue. The "V" must be changed to an "X"; the sermon is where the lines cross. What is behind or above it narrows in to thirty minutes (they are beginning to insist on twenty now) of something said. Its issues widen out as the issues of life widen out.

Sometimes there seems to be no issue at all or only fugitive, trivial issues. People have merely been to church and gone home. They have been entertained, interested, or instructed and that seems the end of it all. Actually they have been helped in ways they cannot make very clear. They have translated what their preacher said into some sustaining hope, have caught through the veil of his words some light to guide them. Their feeble purposes toward good have been strengthened, their infirm wills reinforced, the little fire upon the altars of their devotion quickened into flame. They have found something to go on with for another week.

Nothing of all this is much in itself but widened through all the churches and continued through the years it becomes a tremendous and indispensable force. It may be well or very sadly done but no sermon is without a little gleam. It carries always the implications of vaster horizons, the suggestion of something beyond itself. The plain walls of little churches for a little open out into some transfiguring vision. Life for an hour has become an affair with love and duty, with timeless values and prophetic hopes, and with God. Tides from the great deep wash in and those who feel the awesome wash of them are not afraid. They are the tides of a divine love and power to which we may commit ourselves and be at peace.

I preached a Sunday morning last summer in the little stone church on Appledore (the Isles of Shoals). The island itself was only a little surface of rock lifted out of the bosom of the Atlantic and washed half bare by wind and wave. The church itself was plain as stone could make it. But the feet of vanished generations, always in peril of the sea, had worn a little smooth the granite across which they sought its threshold. The path was only a shadow but it was there. There were only a handful of us within its hallowed walls and what I said was of little moment. The church and the sea and the sky said it all. The walls shut us in to worship, friendship, and prayer, but the windows opened upon the sea with its mystic distances where sea and sky were one, its shining roads to harbors beyond our vision, its summons to enchanted lands of dream and desire. The whole of life was there; its earth and time-bound limitations, its walls of necessity, its windows which open upon the far horizons beyond which our true homeland seems to lie.

Preaching will do little to give meaning to the far horizons unless it give spiritual content to what is near and definite and demanding. When it helps toward the good life and does its own wise, brave part to get about us a good world; when it serves to create an intelligent faith; when it lifts the commonplace to levels of nobler meaning and fits brief days into a vaster pattern, it will always be extending the whole outlook of life. It can do none of these things without relating life to something beyond itself.

Every duty involves a moral order, all love is an inlet from a love more sovereign. The issues of life are always further on. As Dante could not write of Florence truly until he had made her narrow streets lead to the terraces of the Mount of Purgation, the Bolgia of the Inferno, or the singing spheres of the Paradiso, so preaching which begins with what is nearest the pulpit stairs will, if it go far and high enough, end with the practice of the presence of God. There are no horizons beyond that.

CHAPTER X

THE PREACHER'S FORGOTTEN WORD: WITH SOME CONSIDERATION OF CRAFTSMANSHIP

AN ENGLISH preacher of great distinction has recently called homiletics an almost fool-proof art. He did not mean to say that any fool can preach (or, I trust, can teach it) though, curiously enough, most of the preaching in Shakespeare is done by his "fools"—which is worth considering. The poet's task, Matthew Arnold says, is "the noble and profound application of ideas to life . . . under the conditions fixed for them by the laws of poetic beauty and poetic truth." All great poetry, Arnold holds, must have a moral content if morality be so defined that "whatever bears upon the question, How to Live, comes under it." But when the poet begins to "moralize" he ceases to be a poet, although he may in such meditative moments supply the preacher his most treasured quotations.

The dramatist does not need to preach. He creates his situations and his characters according to the veracity of his vision and lets all therein involved work through to the inevitable issue of tragedy or triumph. Shakespeare knew, however, by the sure instinct of genius that there should always be a voice to say to kings what their ministers dare not say, or comment, like the chorus in a Greek tragedy, upon deeds and consequences which the protagonists of the drama, under the compulsion of fateful action, had no time or mind to consider. Only Shakespeare's fools are wise enough or brave enough to do that. Which is, maybe, what St. Paul meant when he spoke of "the foolishness of preaching."

Dr. Rattenbury did not mean that either. He did mean that the construction of a sermon is so essentially simple that "the wayfaring man though a fool need not err therein" unless he puts himself to really a great deal of trouble. Preaching rarely misses the mark through simple directness or want of conscious art. It more generally misses the mark—which is homiletic "sin"—through working too hard, saying too much, and overbuilding its own structure. Preaching suffers from this in the pulpit where it is done, in the classroom where it is taught, and, though this is said cautiously, in the really enormous literature about preaching. It is certainly possible to overteach homiletics and get students into the state of mind of the centipede who, through an excessive preoccupation with his technique, ended in the ditch.*

The liturgies of the ancient church have been defined by the irreverent as devices for getting the clergy into the chancel, occupying them while there and getting them out again decently and in order. This definition applies to many things beside liturgies—including sermons. There are substantially only three movements in any sermon: getting into it, getting

---

* In our work here at Auburn we do a good deal with students who have been preaching, self-taught, before they came to us. Any teacher knows how difficult it is wisely to help a self-taught pupil. There is always a period of almost antagonistic confusion. I have a growing feeling that we occasionally—in the department of preaching—spoil a good man who would best have been left to his own instincts in form and method. He needed very greatly the content of mind the other departments could furnish him and in homiletics a creative criticism which he found it a little hard to take. But he gained little from our formal technique even though we made that so simple as, I should think, to pain the spirits of earlier teachers—some of them great teachers—which haunt in tradition our classroom.

through it, and getting away from it with some clean-cut finality. It would be threshing old straw to go into detail. The laws and principles involved are common to all good public address, and a well-trained mind uses them instinctively.

The sheer effectiveness of many public speakers who have had little formal training proves that a sound, natural sense for saying what one has to say is worth more than semester hours in any classroom on public speaking. The crucial contribution of the classroom is a faculty for self-criticism. Once that has been developed and lodged in the subconscious,* since the subconscious is mostly the seat of its administration, the teacher's work is done. Thereafter he may dismiss his student as Virgil dismissed Dante upon the threshold of the earthy paradise when all the weary terraces of Purgatory had been climbed:

> "Await no more a word or sign from me;
>
> . . . . . .
>
> Wherefore I set on thee miter and crown."

Which is, perhaps, the true end of all education.

Any sermon will keep this ghostly monitor of the preacher busy enough. It will haunt his study desk with an unseen hand upon his pen. It will watch and shape the structure of his sentences in "extempore" preaching. It will anticipate development, warn against detours, put up "No Thoroughfare" signs, and labor manfully and sometimes thanklessly to keep what is being said upon its proper road. When a preacher has nothing to say worth the labor—and this happens to the best of them—his inner control will leave him sadly with a

---

* The psychologist would say, I think, "the foreground subconscious." I have a notion as we get older the "foreground subconscious" gets less creatively responsive, like worked-out soil.

warning to stop as soon as decently may be, and the promise
to come back next Sunday if he will spend brain-sweating
hours in the interval.

Actually this regnant monitor is the deposit of searching
self-discipline. The preacher's habits of study, his reading,
his dominant meditations, his teachableness, and his passion
for his art all combine to create it. It is linked up with the
structure of his mind, his physical state, his years, and deep,
unescapable rhythms of his very being. There are elements
in it beyond his power to create unless they were born with
him, and other elements he can never escape unless he be
reborn. But this deeper self out of which he preaches and
which is the unseen control of all his work can be trained,
enriched, and trusted. When his hour is come it will not
fail him.

I.

The tests of the first movement of a sermon are timing
and mobilization. The preacher has to get himself into his
message and get the congregation with him. Two lines of
approach converge and he has to manage both of them. Half
his introduction is for himself, half for the expectant folk
before him whose more or less wandering minds must be
brought together, stirred to interest, and told what it is all
about. The sooner the preacher and congregation get together
for the business in hand the better. A deal of preaching goes
wrong at the start and never thereafter gets entirely right because these two lines of approach do not meet soon enough
or completely enough. By the time the preacher is through
with his self-starter the congregation are off on their own
lines; some of which would surprise the shepherd of their
souls.

The preacher should do his self-starting in the study. There he can write and cross out, throw false starts into the waste-basket, think and begin again. Even the best disciplined minds must go through a process of exploration before they discover the dominant association lines of any text or theme and see a shining road open before them. They do not need to take their waste-baskets into the pulpit or their tentative explorations either. The real introduction to a sermon is often, as far as the preacher is concerned, well down in his manu-script, his notes, or what he has been thinking out and think-ing over. He may be compelled in beginning where he should to leave out sentences he has caressed or paragraphs he has lovingly labored. They never will be missed, being only what he needed to get his own mind in strong, direct action.

Once he is in the pulpit, his main concern is the mobiliza-tion of the attention and interest of the congregation. Some men do this instinctively. They have a sure sense of crowd-psychology and accomplish without conscious analysis what the psychologist can make a long chapter of. Most preachers need to study that art. If there are essentially three move-ments in a sermon the first danger is that the approach should be too long and too wandering.

The second movement is the organized and developed say-ing of what the sermon sets out to say. About this also the preacher can find any amount of good advice. He can build a sermon as a mason builds a wall; organize it around his sequence of "firstlys," "secondlys," and so on. He may use the time-honored technique of thesis, antithesis, and syn-thesis; make a symphony of it, if he can, with Beethoven-like developments of his theme; or grow it as a tree grows with trunk and branches spreading into a wealth of foliation through which the lights and shadows play and the winds make music. This last is essentially the essayist's art and the secret of full development. It is easy enough to grow a homiletic trunk with a few main, bare branches in the air, like the trees we used to see in the battle areas, but to carry a branch through all its aspiring finials to the full-finished spread of it is another matter and far more difficult.*

Whatever method of organization is used the true development is in the very structure of the matter. There are alternative roads through most themes and texts, but there is always one road determined by what is essential and inevitable in the unfolding of their truth and meaning. It is *there*, as the contours of the hills and valleys of a region are *there* for road builders. The engineer does not make them. They are given and there is only one entirely right road through them. The test of the surveyor's plot and the engineer's skill is to find this already earth-made road and follow it. This is also the test of the preacher's skill, though the lines he has to follow are truth-made and vision-built. They are more than logic and resource; they are in the deep necessity, the pregnant nature of his message.

Once he finds the one inevitable line of development, the rest is easy. The sermon will organize itself; as he goes on he will find what is to be said next waiting for him because it must be said next. He will be wise to make the stages of his journey plain to his people. This will give them something to lay hold of and recollect; as though a traveler should remember his journey by the towns through which he passed, the rivers he crossed, the hilltops from which he saw a gracious valley and, beyond, another range of hills.

These memories bring both a sermon and a map alive. All noble preaching has this inevitable quality as all noble writing

---

* Our students commonly bring in sermon outlines with "points" enough for a month's preaching. They find it easier to add another point than develop what they have written down. That does not, I imagine, end with the seminary. Under-development and over-pointing are the perils of extempore preaching.

has it and commanding speech upon any theme. Once the preacher has thought these roads through, traveled them in his own mind till he knows them as a man knows the roads he has walked again and again, he will not, I am persuaded, need to take any guide-posts with him (in the shape of notes) into the pulpit.

He has only to set out anew and take his congregation with him. As he goes on what comes next will be waiting. He will not so much remember it as rediscover it. There will be variations of course since no road is ever twice the same. He will miss what he meant to say and say with creative passion what he had not thought to say. These passages kindled by immediate action have a contagious power. They are a fire which fuses with a shared flame the speaker and the audience. But always his progress is in the crescent emergence of his thought, his ascent from level to waiting level, the drive through of what he says upon its predetermined conclusions. It is for him a journey made new by the enthusiasm of sharing it; it is discovery, surprise, and consent for the congregation. When it is done as now and then every preacher does, there will be at the end a half heard sigh as of regret that it is over, as of wonder that it could have been.

II.

That blessed wonder, if the preacher win the tribute of it, depends crucially upon the last movement of the sermon, or else the sigh will be a sigh of relief and the congregation will go home with an unhappy sense of having been nowhere but to church. The last movement is not the rhetorician's peroration or the text-book's conclusion. It is as much as anything else the way in which a sermon draws in upon life. This is not saying that every sermon ought to end with an exhortation or even with a concrete application. It does mean that what has been said must reach and rest upon some definite frontier of thought, faith, or conduct and that it must not leave an unbridged gap between itself and the possible issue of it in life.

Contemporaneous preaching is entirely adequate in quality of thought, range of idealism, resource, and sincerity. Preaching is probably stronger in all these elements than at any time in its history, but it is facing a situation it has not faced so crucially since Peter preached on the Day of Pentecost. It is facing the question point, "how?" That is rampant against all our horizons—political, social, financial, international.

No epoch has ever really wanted so many entirely desirable and defensible things as ours. It wants international peace—at least the inarticulate commons of all nations do. It wants security, economic well-being, and fulness of life. It wants knowledge. It cannot endure an unweighed star or an atom which will not disclose the secret of its being. It wants to know about human nature, to discover the sources and laws of our being and to plumb all the depths of our souls, and it is asking "how?" "how?" "how?" There is not an aspect of our enormous experimentation in every field of life which, when we see it stripped bare, is not a question mark in tumultuous and murky action.

"How" is also the master question for Christianity and Christian preaching. "*How* can we know God?" "*How* can we be Christians?" "*How* can we realize a Christian world?" "*How* can we deal with our faults and failures?" "*How* can we meet sorrow, loss, and pain victoriously?" "*How* can prayer be answered?" "*How* can we be saved?" "*How* can our religion become a reality other than words?" "*How* can the nostalgias of our spirits be satisfied and the ladder of our dreams be so set upon our rough earth-ways that we can use their rungs to climb by and not find them break beneath our feet?"

The old answers will not do. Reality has gone out of them, at least the reality which the temper of our time demands. Protestantism needs a new technique of the religious life, needs, in plain words, a "how" of the Christian life fitted to the temper of the time and drawing to the full upon every contribution to our knoweldge of ourselves and our world. Now most sermons face this whole demanding situation in their last movement. The preacher has made his case, developed his proposition, indicated a duty, or promised a blessing—what you please. He needs to take a care, for whose importance I can find no adjective, that, as all this draws in upon life as it is just then and there before him, he does not lose himself and his congregation in a holy obscurity of pious phrases and exhortations. *The preacher's forgotten word is "how."*

And why? Well because it is so difficult, so demanding, because, perhaps, he does not know himself. Because a glowing peroration like charity covers a multitude of (homiletic) sins. Because "how" brings him down out of the clouds. Because even for him realism and religion seem to belong to different worlds. So a deal of preaching no matter where it starts or where it said it was going when it started ends in a golden glow of time-hallowed phrases. When the glow darkens "how?" begins to show again. I do not say it is left wholely unanswered but that too often it is left far more vaguely answered than even the difficulty of answering can justify. This is due in part to a habit preachers—especially extemporaneous preachers—frankly confess. They spend too much time in too long introductions but the first third of their sermons they do prepare carefully.*

The second third they "block out" on broad lines and trust their mounting mental and emotional action to fill with definite

* This is the substance of a heart-to-heart talk between the members of the Wranglers Club in Detroit, nearly all of whom were "extempore" preachers of more than ordinary force.

kindling content the spaces they have left open. The last and vital movement they do no more than hopefully survey, trusting to be carried through by some tide of inspiration and their own adroitness. Sometimes the tides they wait for come full flood with an oceanic amplitude behind them. Quite as often—or oftener—the tide ebbs and leaves the sermon stranded. There can be only one control for this—two-thirds of a preacher's labor should be upon the last third of a sermon. He must study proportion, not waste in his approach the five or ten minutes he will need so urgently as his sermon draws in upon its meanings, direct or indirect, for life. He will not wisely propose more in his main developments than he can dispose of, nor suggest problems upon whose solution he can throw no light.

There is a place for challenging preaching, which leaves issues for which it has no immediate solution to God and time. Such preaching at least keeps the congregation awake. But too much of it weighs the congregation down beneath a burden which they may eventually escape by the simple device of staying at home Sundays. We are at present so sadly conscious of our difficulties and entanglements as to make it quite unnecessary for a preacher to begin every Sunday's sermons with a résumé of them. He will do best at present if he begins with "how" and ends with an answer even if it be tentative enough. The best preaching today is taking exactly this line. It lays hold of some one of all the urgent, pathetic, and often unvoiced appeals for help which, like autumnal spiders' webs, are flung abroad to find something to lay hold of, and meets it with a positive contribution.

Such preaching is not easy. It must get at the roots of need in the soul and society. It will not be content with mere palliatives. Creative help is more than today's courage or tomorrow's hope, though for us who can so often see no further than tomorrow and can do no more than pray, "Give us today our daily courage," such preaching has an invaluable office. But help is understanding and disentanglement, it is "why" as well as "how," light as well as heat. It does not stop with consequences; it seeks for causes. It diagnoses our sicknesses only to furnish them some cure which reaches the seat of the disorder. It probes our wounds to remove the source of irritation. Help is far-visioned; it builds constructive programs, it is idealistic in its ends, realistic in its methods. It does not expect too much too soon. It knows that some element of failure will attend the noblest enterprises. It never asks for all or nothing, welcomes any cooperation, never carries all its traffic on one track.

It is not afraid of the Valley of Humiliation, takes the Hill of Difficulty bravely, finds the keys to deliver us from Doubting Castle and Giant Despair. And it knows that no healing is complete till the soul is cured nor anything radically changed till life is changed. Preaching has always been charged with a gospel of help; the gospel would not be "good news" unless it did bring help. Its mandate was never more clear or crucial than now. The minor aspects of the technique of a well-made sermon are entirely subordinate to the splendor of this task. Noble preaching always fuses its elements in its truth and passion. When it is drawn from living fires it will find its proper molds.

III.

All this has to be done with words. Not with words alone: for nothing is ever entirely done with words, but neither is anything of account ever entirely done without words. There are, no need to say it, "songs without words" and great, silent though speaking, canvases. There are recitatives in stone and the wordless message of timeless deeds, yet even these need words to interpret or record them. They need words about them before they are complete. Words have never lost the childlike wonder with which our race, learning to speak, hailed its own achievement. It is as though when the eonian travail of the inarticulate spirit which was becoming man was accomplished and a word was born, the morning stars sang together because the soul at last was free.

So words were invested with a magic power. The very saying of them did something. If only one could find the proper word he might accomplish anything—cure a sickness, crush a foe, or, if the word were secret and powerful enough, shake the earth. This magic of the dawn of speech has been sublimated but never lost. Words are ships to carry the commerce of our spirits. They cross the seas of silence and of time. One does not see the snow fall without remembering the words of Odysseus "like wintry snowflakes," nor read the translation of a Chaldean tablet without some sense of nearness to cities turned to dust. A word may start a crusade, redate history, mobilize an army, immortalize a statesman, plight a love, or change a destiny:

> "One man with a dream, at pleasure
> Shall go forth and conquer a crown;
> And three with a new song's measure
> Can trample an empire down."

But the dream must be made articulate and the song is only singing speech.

The preacher's words, then, are his instruments, his peril, and his power. There are things enough one may say about them but this is, maybe, most important; that they should come out of life and be changeable back into life. Preaching has a great inheritance of words. Some of them are the noblest words of which speech is capable—the creation of Christian faith and thought. Some of them have been packed with meaning through sequent centuries, some have been worn smooth by much handling. A preacher's words may become a nest of boxes, an inept figure, out of which he can keep taking other words till he has a pile of words. He may use them as a magician's hat out of which surprising things can be taken which were never really there at all. The best figure, I think, is a head of wheat into which has gone seed-germ, soil-gifts, sun-quickening, and the ministry of the seasons. All that has combined to make them is in them but they cannot be entirely understood, root and all, branch and all, unless their meaning is found in their growth.

Many of the preacher's inherited words are out-moded. They are, as Henry Sloane Coffin says, like coins which need to be withdrawn from circulation, reminted, and reissued. It is not so much a matter of finding synonyms for them, as of finding living vehicles for the living minds of the burning present. If the words of religion become static they will not furnish religion a free channel thorugh which to flow. Some of them must always be words any dictionary will find it hard to define. A definition is really a fence and words which can be precisely fenced in, though extremely useful for the logician and scientist, do not serve the needs of the poet or the theologian. We need words open to the uses of the imagination, to the faculties of awe and wonder, far-horizoned words, plastic to suggestion.

The true meaning of many very simple words like "life" and "love" and "duty" is not in what they say but what they suggest. What possible correspondence can there be between Spencer's ponderous definition of life and a June meadow, the moonlit ecstacy of a mocking bird, the laughter of a child or our own strange pilgrimages through the years? It is as impossible to give a precise definition to love as to hold within any fenced field the cloud shadows which drift across it or the winds which wash into waves the gold of ripened grain.

The greatest words of religion belong of necessity to this high fellowship. They can do no more than suggest some aspect of the infinite mystery and yet it is the preacher's task to give them some meaning for reason to lay hold of and experience to take and use. On the other hand they may easily become escape words. Nearly every preacher will find, if he watch his work, that he has cherished phrases which he uses just where the necessity of thoughtful and more precise development is most urgent and he does not know how to manage it. They are mostly adjectives: "infinite," "absolute," "eternal," "unseen," "omnipotent." He cannot entirely do without them but they may easily become smoke screens behind which he disappears when his flight has become too high or hazardous. There is reality in them but they ought never to be used as an escape from reality. One can build an awesome structure of them but he needs to look to his foundations.

IV.

No matter how high and grandly—or grandiosely—speculation builds its structure and no matter how it names it, what is so built finally makes its contacts with reality at three points. They are experience, observation, and the funded experience of the past we call history. "Point" is too limited a word but it will do. Experience is anything from an aching tooth to the poet's rapture over daffodils and the mystic's sense of God. Observation is anything from the sight of snowflakes drifting through pallid March sunshine to moral insight. History is anything from the date of a battle to such records as we have of the entire human enterprise. But everything we dream or believe or know or create takes its departure from these three points, and must in the end come back to them.

If in another order we shall know more clearly:

> "The truths that never can be proved
> Until we close with all we loved,
> And all we flow from, soul in soul,"

it will be because we shall have a new wealth of experience and changed faculties of observation. This teacher of preaching, and sometime preacher, wishes he knew how to say all this clearly and strongly. If he had been more critical of his own word-fabrics it would have been well. They are so easy to create. They may so easily become ends in themselves, so easily escape these three controls. He does not know any correction of any kind of unreality in speech or thought so definite as the honest use of plain words to carry meaning and not to confuse emotion.*

The words of meaningful human use are never too far above the levels of daily human life. These are the best words for the preacher. He may always wisely ask himself what would happen if he were to forego his favorite adjectives, or if all that he says were passed through a screen meshed to sift out all words over three syllables. Or what would happen if his words were cooler to the touch.

This writer does not under-estimate the value of style which is always the living texture of any speech. Nor does he under estimate the attention-compelling quality of heightened speech vividly said. There are always lines of thought which as they rise to noble levels take on an amplitude of expression for which only the great words are sufficient. But this must always come from the inside and under compulsion; just as a teacher once tied together, with not too easily breakable cord, the hands of a singer much given to gesture, and waited for the true passion of the song to break the cord. It is no easy task to say a great thing simply or use the words nearest our dusty ways to lift us above their dust. But the words which are nearest to life are commonly the more simple words. They inform and command,

---

* Interesting to note that some of our neo-realists are building for themselves a structure too much of which turns out upon examination to be a highly speculative vocabulary impressively used.

they plead or reprieve, they sing or sigh and march, they are nobly luminous.

They have been shaped by human nature's daily use and so are never far from our familiar ways. If an artist use them, they are capable of saying most of what we know enough to say. Jesus used the words of the household, the carpenter shop, the farmer, and the merchant. There was nothing He had to say of God or man or destiny for which they were not sufficient. Such words are best suited to nervous directness of movement and, since they have been shaped through immemorial use, they lend themselves to rhythm and may become the noblest of music.*

They are the poet's own words. He makes of them his greatest lines: as though when like a skylark he sings half lost in light, the words which come down cannot be native to the sky unless they were first native to earth. John Bunyan found them enough to tell the story of Christian's Pilgrim-Progress and enough to get Mr. Valiant-For-Truth across the river while "all the trumpets sounded for him on the other side."

They may become all this for the preacher if he can manage it and they will, besides, keep him near to life. He must be on guard against flight words and, though he cannot preach without faith words, he can do most of what he has to do without speculation words. So his words become by a deep necessity a test and a control. Any sermon built with a speculative or unusual vocabulary, no matter how impressively used, is being

---

* The words of Socrates were also, according to Alcibiades, simple and homely. "They are ridiculous when you first hear them; . . . for his talk is of pack-asses and smiths and cobblers and curriers, and he is always repeating the same things in the same words, so that any ignorant or inexperienced person might feel disposed to laugh at him; but he who . . . sees what is within will find that they are the only words which have a meaning in them, and also the most divine, abounding in fair images of virtue, and of the widest comprehension, or rather extending to the whole duty of a good and honorable man."

built away from life. Being wise, he will not, of course, use words most people do not understand or make of any sermon a verbal soufflé. He will be sensitive, through his own faculty of self-criticism, to thick, opaque passages in writing or speech. Half a dozen opaque lines will cloud any page; three or four "thick" paragraphs undo any sermon.

They are usually due to confusion of thought or else to something over-said or written. Punctuation will help; breaking up a long sentence will help; and words which let the light through will help most of all. A good deal of preaching is like the opalescent glass with which at one time church windows were filled. They were well enough but the general result was a holy gloom. The men who built Amiens and Sainte Chapelle had a better art. The light came through their glass in multi-colored glory but it came as light. Some words are impervious to actinic rays; they are rarely missed when gone. Very often the only cure for a "thick" passage is to cut it out altogether. It also will rarely be missed.

Finally, in his use of words the preacher cannot go far wrong is he uses words which are native to the structure of his own mind and serve his own thought processes naturally. A preacher can no more use another preacher's style than he can wear his clothes. The style is the man. There is even a relation between one's sentence rhythm and one's breath rhythm. Usually in extempore preaching this manages itself. The speaker learns, in time, to end his sentences before he runs out of breath to say them with. But it is easily possible to ignore this control in writing. Result: long and involved sentences which cannot be read naturally and are panted out, or else, being unsupported by sustained breath, get lost at the end. A wise teacher puts the correction in four words: "Hit the last word." But how can one "hit the last word" if his breath gives out before he reaches it?

V.

Few sermons demand the entire attention of the listener. An agile listening mind, so Dr. Oliver Wendell Holmes maintained, can circle about a sermon much as a king-bird around a crow, and he developed that quaint conceit delightfully. The flaw in the Autocrat's analogy is that occasionally the agile mind goes off entirely on its own flights, and like Noah's dove does not come back, or else folds its wings and goes to sleep. An intelligent listener does not need more than half his mind half the time actually to follow the argument of a quite soundly reasoned sermon and anticipate its conclusions. The listener is thus left too much to his own devices,* with resultant wanderings of mind from which, among other things, a collect beseeches the good Lord to deliver us. On the other hand, if the sermon demand an over-strained attention, it may attract what is called "an intelligent congregation," but there are likely to be vacant pews in the church. If preaching is to attract and hold a congregation it must be interesting. The average listener would grade interest at 66-2/3 as against 33-1/3 for solid wisdom in marking any sermon up to par.

Preachers are not likely to appreciate how vital interest is until, through some change of occupation, they begin to listen to sermons themselves.† The speaker, it has been suggested, is self-hypnotized. The faces of his auditors become a blur, the external world fades, the flight of time is unheeded, nothing is

---

* A frank parishioner of mine once told me he liked going to church. If he heard anything he cared for he listened. If not, he considered his own affairs. "I once," he said, "got an idea in church which was worth $10,000 to me." It was not a wasted hour.

† Preachers should from time to time be given leave-of-absence to be spent not in Russia but in the pews of average churches. They would come back to their own pulpits with an understanding sympathy for their own congregations which would be highly useful.

real except the spell out of which he speaks.* There is, one suspects, a measure of truth in this. Public speaking is an engrossing occupation and always has a high interest content for the person who is doing it. His interest in his own work may lead him not to take pains enough to make it interesting to the congregation or to consider whether it bears at all upon their situation.

The preacher is often interested in subjects about which the congregation are not much concerned. He may be working through a phase of religious thought or personal adjustment which the pews do not share. His battles are not always their battles; he may be carrying on some engagement behind the pulpit with an adversary they cannot see, with an ardor they cannot account for. They cannot kindle their fires from his. What he is doing may be highly significant but badly timed. Colonel Lindbergh's father, we now hear, anticipated aspects of the NRA but got nothing for it save the reputation of being a "crank" Congressman. It has been often enough the tragedy of the far-visioned to have been consumed by a fire which left the world cold when, in after time, it would have kindled a mighty flame.

The first condition of an interesting sermon is, then, a fused unity interest for both preacher and congregation. He may be on fire with what has little interest for them. Result: heat in the pulpit and coldness in the pews. They may be intensely interested in regions which leave him cold. Result: a dissatisfied or unhelped congregation. A preacher will never be on fire with a message unless it gets hold of him entirely. A congregation will not respond unless it reaches them.

---

* Public speech may also do something like hypnotism for the audience. A very self-restrained man told me once of hearing Bishop Simpson during the Civil War. At the end of the address, he said, he found himself pounding his umbrella on the platform and he added: "I did not know how I got there."

This unreconciled play of interests is responsible for the unhappy issue of many pastorates. The power to fuse his own
interest with the interest of the congregation is a gift and an
instinct. Our most effective preachers do it with a deep sureness. They work with flowing tides whose direction and force
they have first felt themselves. This has been the secret of
the statesman's power as well as the preacher's regnancy over
a congregation or an epoch. It is a priceless gift but it is not
beyond any preacher's power to attain in some measure.

The second condition of interest content is the whole action
of the preacher. So called "extempore preaching" possesses a
great advantage here, for the congregation see a process of
creation going on before them.* They travel with the preacher's
exploratory mind. They share his search for words, they see the
premonitory flush of rising passion on his face. They hear in
his voice the changing stresses of his mind and emotion. Here
is one secret of the long ascendency of public address over the
popular imagination. When the full power of a great mind in
immediate action upon an adequate theme and under the challenge of a kindling situation is released, the result is a demonstration of a great human faculty. The preacher then shares
with the poet a birthright in that magic realm where out of
the unseen the enduring is created. He also becomes a "maker."

The actor knows how to invest his part with an interest appeal
to which his art, his personality, and his action all contribute.
No line is immaterial, no word neglected. His stage is often a
place of tawdry device, his lines banal till he has said them.
But if he be master of his art, great issues seem to be afoot
through his painted show of things and his voice plucks at the
heart strings. When a preacher begins to act (of design) some-

---

* People will stop to see anything made. Witness the crowds at a
shop window with a process of manufacture inside—or the centers of
popular interest at the "Century of Progress."

thing begins to be lost and there remains at last only a technique through which the artifice shows. But a preacher may take account of the elements of interest content which are due to his own personal action for all that.

VI.

The most dependable interest factor is *movement*,* movement of developing thought. As long as a sermon is going somewhere the congregation will go with it. They do not ask a too one-track movement; *au contraire*. They love such variations of the motif as a musician introduces. They respond happily to detours through a little quiet space of beauty or to some summit of commanding vision but they want always to move on and forward. They share, not always consciously, the preacher's periods of groping uncertainty, get lost with him and do not always get back on the main road with him. Directly the sermon begins to double back their interest weakens. If at the end they are where they started they know that nothing has been done and grudge their wasted time.

The psychologist can add his own long list to the elements of interest in any sermon. He would make much of suspended expectation, not too long suspended. Surprise is vital, the right kind of surprise. An alert mind usually anticipates the end of a sentence or an argument. If it is quite sure of the issue it goes about its own affairs. Any preacher must take care if he do not fall into speech-ways and phrase-ways which his congregation know too well to care to follow. He must take more care if he do not fall into deeply trodden thought-ways. He needs from time to time to move into some new region of ruling ideas. Almost any pulpit Bible opens of itself upon worn pages, so does almost any study Bible. Most preachers can create a

---

* People will watch any moving object till it stops. Then they look around for something else.

new interest for themselves and the congregation by getting a fresh range of texts. There are texts enough.

Illustration—vivid, dramatic, moving illustration—is a telling element in preaching. It makes it human, alive. Illustration usually gets a chapter by itself in the books. It cannot be considered in a paragraph save to say that it demands imagination, a sure sense of analogy, good taste, a mind always open to suggestion, and a constant accumulation of illustrative material. The sources of illustration are as various as nature, literature, history, life, science, and all the arts. Those nearest our own thresholds are best. They should never be purple patches on a fustian garment or, indeed, patches at all. They should never demand more background than the congregation possesses. They do best when the sermon passes into illustration and out again without a detour. Dr. Henry Howard had an unusual gift for the use of illustrations and analogies from science. He made them with a rare art a part of the very structure of his preaching. They supplied interest, illustration, and substance and became one secret of his deserved popularity.

Quotations are a very present help in time of trouble. They lend authority to the sermon, certify to the preacher's erudition and range of reading, and, occasionally, awe the congregation. They may also say what a preacher wants to say better than he can say it himself. The late Henry Churchill King—one of the finest minds of his generation—always quoted generously and to the point. So did Washington Gladden. The demanding and unreasonable forms copyright laws have recently taken make quotation in published sermons either hazardous or a tiresome affair of getting permissions.*

---

* Book after book is being published now which owe the bulk of their content to the use of published material and then forbid the use of their own material "in any form." It all seems very much like building a series of little copyrighted dams across the free current of human thought.

Poetic quotation had for a while an excessive vogue. Sermons became anthologies and were now and then obviously directed toward the recitation of a poem as their reason for being preached at all. As long as such quotation was an evidence of the preacher's ripened friendship with the poets it had its own power. Now that "anthologies" supply a cross-indexed catalogue of song for every conceivable occasion, it has become too easy and our more original minds are giving it up. Since the poet, however, has always said in a final and perfect way so much the preacher seeks to say and cannot, a quotation may become more than mere quotation. It may be the brief and inevitable conclusion, lyric and light-touched, of what he seeks to say, or else furnish wings to cross a deep abyss, or a grave music to move the heart.

Many preachers use application instead of illustration. They bring their message down to life situations and quicken it with meanings which the hearer takes home to his own hearthstone, his own tasks, or his own soul. Such preaching may be poor in illustration; it is electric with contacts and charged with power. It is, I venture to believe, the kind of preaching which will best serve our time whose Christian task is to bring the Way, the Truth, and the Life of Jesus Christ to bear on the whole of life. The applications of the gospel begin with the imaginations of our hearts, they reach through all the unordered foregrounds of all our shared life, they include the heights of faith, they touch with light the horizons of our holiest hopes. Whoever brings them to bear with creative power upon any aspect of life can be sure of answering interest.

VII.

By such tests as these preaching may become an art, a very noble art, never right until it is an art. "Art," said Browning in *The Ring and the Book,* "remains the one way possible of speaking truth—at least for me." The preacher may speak truth and be no artist but his truth will tell and carry in proportion to the art of it for art is supreme excellence in any action, creation, or expression. It is rooted in skill. It grows through discipline. It rises through creative levels. It has its altars and its seven-branched candlestick. It issues in as near perfection as lies within our mortal power and becomes in words or stone, in music or in color some revealing of God the Creator in man the artifex.

The preacher may be, along with the poet, an artist in words, sensitive to their music and their overtones, their meanings. He should be skilled in fundamental clarities and add thereto rhythm and a texture to catch the light and husband little shadows. He must be, with the painter, an artist in subject and composition, his lines converge upon what is most significant, his highlights fall where their incidence is inevitable. Like the painter he also should make his empty spaces contributory to the picture, neither forgetting color nor mishandling it. He must use form as the sculptor and imagination as the dramatist. He is comrade to the architect though he use an imponderable material.* The beauty he seeks is the beauty of holiness, the art he would perfect is the art of life so lived in time as to be shaped for the timeless. And all his other arts will lack their final power unless he be himself deeply versed in the art of the practice of the presence of God and know how to share it with his people.

No sermon is ever all of this. Now and then some gleam of final excellence comes through any sermon, in the music of words, in a sequence of great utterance, in an insight or a

---

* See John Ruskin—*Seven Lamps of Architecture*—the whole of it. It bears directly with a wealth of illustration upon what is fundamental in law and method in the art of preaching.

foresight, in some unforgettable accent of the Holy Ghost, in some way with life to lift it to its true home. Preaching on these levels, though they be not continuously maintained, need not apologize to any art. It may teach them all the source of their own excellences and reveal to them the ends they are meant to serve.